NATURALLY SALTY

Naturally Salty

Coastal Characters of the Pacific Northwest

Marianne Scott

TouchWood Editions

VICTORIA • VANCOUVER

TouchWood Editions Ltd.
Victoria, BC, Canada
This book is distributed by The Heritage Group, #108-17665 66A Avenue, Surrey, BC, Canada, V3S 2A7.

Cover design by Pat McCallum; book design and layout by Retta Moorman.
Cover photographs: Tourism British Columbia (front); Marianne Scott (insets front and back).

This book is set in Goudy Old Style.

TouchWood Editions acknowledges the financial support for its publishing program from the Canada Council for the Arts, the Government of Canada through the Book Publishing Industry Development Program (BPIDP) and the Province of British Columbia through the British Columbia Arts Council.

Printed and bound in Canada by Friesens, Altona, Manitoba.

National Library of Canada Cataloguing in Publication Data

Scott, Marianne, 1942-
  Naturally salty: coastal characters of the Pacific Northwest / Marianne Scott.

ISBN 1-894898-03-6

1. Boats and boating—Northwest, Pacific—Biography. 2. Northwest, Pacific—Biography. I. Title.
GV776.N76S36 2003   797.1'09795   C2003-910334-X

BRITISH
COLUMBIA
ARTS COUNCIL
Supported by the Province of British Columbia

The Canada Council | Le Conseil des Arts
for the Arts | du Canada

To David

who helped me rediscover my salty roots

Contents

Introduction

I wonder if people whose lives are linked to the sea are more interesting than those who inhabit landlocked places, or if it just seems that way. Maybe life on or at the edges of salt water attracts those who are more adventurous, daring or curious. What I know for sure is that the individuals whom I have had the privilege to interview up and down the coasts of British Columbia and Washington lead varied, fascinating and fulfilling existences.

I came to write this book after a long hiatus from my own salty background. My childhood and early teens in the Netherlands were, perforce, water drenched. More than half of that country lies below sea level, and only a series of dunes and dikes keeps the land from drowning. The lowlands are a huge watershed for the Rhine and Meuse rivers and their tributaries. When I was a girl, my brother, Frank, and I would tramp through the meadows next to a highway near Rotterdam and catch salamanders and polliwogs in the shallow drainage ditches that carved the green grass into tidy squares. During our after-church, Sunday-afternoon strolls, my father usually took us walking along the Schie, a small river that connects Rotterdam and Delft, and we'd look at the tugs, barges and other workboats, many of which housed their skippers and their families. In front of our second-storey house, a *singel*, one of the ubiquitous canal-like stretches of water that drain the moisture ceaselessly accumulating in the flat landscape, offered a great ice-skating rink in the winter. All that water runs into the turbulent, dangerous North Sea, which has shaped Holland's history as a seafaring and mercantile nation.

My grandfather earned his living as a loadmaster for ocean-going freighters that loaded and discharged their cargoes in the Rotterdam harbours. One of his tasks was to ensure that ships were not overloaded and that their cargoes were stowed properly so that a violent seaway could not unbalance the ship. When he was young, my father, too, worked for export companies in the harbours. My uncle was a marine pilot. We children took our maritime environment for granted — it was part of our daily scene.

After emigrating to a landlocked portion of Ohio, overcoming culture shock and learning English, we didn't consciously miss the rivers, canals and harbours, just the swimming pools. It was only after I moved to Toronto and met David Scott, owner of a sailboat, that I was reintroduced to my watery heritage.

David jokes frequently that my liking to sail was a prerequisite for marriage. Fortunately, I took to it like the proverbial duck to water. We crossed Lake Ontario from Toronto, transited the Erie Barge Canal, Hudson River and Long Island Sound to Massachusetts, and thence to Maine. After moving to Victoria, we explored the straits and sounds of British Columbia and Washington, thus allowing me to appreciate the coastal waters of both countries in which I hold citizenship. In 1996–97, we sailed to Bora Bora and back on our Niagara 35, *Starkindred*, a glorious voyage that, despite our modern conveniences and a GPS, gave me at least a taste of what old seafarers endured. It was during these journeys that I met more and more salty characters — people from around the world, cautious and adventurous, rich, poor and in-between, but all folks whose lives were deeply influenced by the sea. Their stories were fascinating, sometimes spellbinding. Some people were quirky, others solemn; some were gregarious talkers, others only slowly revealed their essence.

These people and my personal experiences inspired me to write articles for yachting magazines. Eventually, Duart Snow, then editor of *Pacific Yachting*, encouraged me to start a regular column showcasing coastal characters in the Pacific Northwest. Some of the people included in *Naturally Salty* were first featured, in shorter form, in the pages of that magazine. Readers sent me suggestions of other beguiling personalities to interview and thus grew the idea for a book chronicling the lives of some of our salt-soaked west coasters.

Getting to know the 31 people in this book has been a joy. These portraits depict adventurers, curmudgeons, writers, artists, highly capable artisans, oddballs, boat designers and builders, sailors and powerboaters. Their ages range from 30 to 88. Their salty interests may diverge, but their love of the sea binds them together. They exhibit many of the same characteristics: curiosity, the ability to make do and the willingness to work hard. If I were to choose one trait they all share, it would be self-reliance.

I sincerely thank all the people who populate this book, who generously gave me their time and invited me into their homes, lives and confidence. Thanks go to all those who sent me names and introduced me to more salty characters. I gratefully acknowledge Duart Snow and Simon Hill, former editors at *Pacific Yachting*, for giving me the opportunity to present some of these biographies in the magazine. My gratitude goes to my writing buddy, Katherine Gibson, always ready with a sharp, red pencil and a kind word. I thank Steve Pridgeon for his pithy titles when I was stuck. I am indebted to Pauline Dawe for transcribing many hours of wandering, taped talk. I am deeply appreciative of Marlyn Horsdal for editing the manuscript, correcting errors and smoothing the flow. And, of course, I thank David Scott, my partner-in-life, my first-cut editor, who cheerfully and frequently sailed off with me in *Starkindred* so I could meet the people in this book.

Marianne Scott
Victoria
February 2003

the sea as calling

Bruce Taylor
the deliverer

Captain Bruce Taylor looks the part. No stained overalls. No ground fibreglass dust coating a worn plaid shirt. No sawdust clinging to his workpants. Instead, a Guernsey sweater tops his navy slacks; a matching dark blue, knit cap completes the ensemble. A handsome white beard and a full head of curly hair, complemented by a diamond stud in his left earlobe with a wee gold shackle just below it, give Bruce a somewhat piratical look. But his competent manoeuvring of the 58-foot West Bay powerboat and intense concentration indicate he's shipshape and in good trim. Those traits, he believes, have made his profession — as delivery skipper and as captain of other people's yachts — a success.

We're aboard a new, raised-pilothouse motor yacht, *La Pituca* (Spanish for "elegant lady"), worth about US$1.5 million. Her pristine carpeting is covered with transparent plastic; everything about the vessel sparkles. I smell the aroma of new, unsullied materials. On the bridge, the electronic charts integrated with the GPS and radar show today's route. Bruce starts the twin 825-horsepower Detroit Diesel engines, engages the vessel's dual props and bow thrusters and, ever so gently, reverses her from a Fraser River dock near Vancouver. He's readied the yacht for her voyage down the west coast, through the Panama Canal and the Caribbean Sea to Fort Lauderdale. But not on her own bottom. *La Pituca* will travel aboard Dockwise's semi-submersible yacht carrier, *Super Servant 3*, registered in Rotterdam. Bruce will deliver the yacht to the Dutch ship awaiting us in Vancouver's Coal Harbour. During the voyage, he will sleep in the yacht's aft stateroom with its queen-size bed; his robe hangs neatly from a hook. A long row of fat adventure novels will provide entertainment while he's at sea.

We glide along the Fraser's south arm at five knots, Bruce's eyes riveted on dozens of floating logs capable of damaging, if not bayoneting, the hull. "My father always told me, 'Never go where the seagulls walk,'" he says with a chuckle. Once in the Strait of Georgia we whoosh along at 20 knots, the boat's wipers whipping aside the salt water pummelling the windshield. Burrard Inlet, then Vancouver Harbour, sparkle calmly, the encircling, snow-dusted mountains resplendent against the azure sky.

While we await our slot in the floating transport, Bruce gives me a snapshot of his life as a skipper of other people's boats and describes bringing a dozen yachts to Idaho's Snake River. "Because of bridges and overpasses, oversized loads cannot be transported east over the Cascades," he explains. So each time he and a mate took one of the delivery vessels down the Washington coast — those 140 miles are usually the toughest part — they crossed the Columbia River bar at high-slack, travelled 300 miles upriver, then another 165 up the Snake to Clarkston, Washington. Eight locks — one with a 90-foot lift — raised them 765 feet above sea level. There, the vessel, which can't exceed 20 feet in height and width, was loaded onto a truck. The "oversized load" followed a back roads route (without overpasses) developed by the U.S. Department of Defense for its missile transports. Bruce loves the Columbia River voyage for its succession of landscapes — rain forests followed by gorge topography, orchards, high desert and then sagebrush and sand.

The loading master's voice, revealing his Netherlandish origins, orders the circling yachts to enter the transporter's open transom one by one. A special CAD program has mapped out the location of each of the 12 motor yachts to be stowed aboard. We decide that when the loading master calls for *La Pituca*'s entry, I'll respond in Dutch (my native language) to his directive and, perhaps, surprise him. Not a chance. The loader switches languages without missing a beat and Bruce nudges us in slowly between a mega-yacht and another 58-footer, beefy fenders dangling to cushion the slightest thump. Divers clad in heavy-duty wetsuits and carrying air tanks guide the yacht into a keel block and place chock stands under the hull. Tomorrow, the ship will rise after blowing her tanks, and each yacht will be tension-strapped to the deck. Heavy marine-grade electrical cords will be strung aboard to top up the batteries and eventually provide air conditioning.

Over the next three weeks, Bruce will keep *La Pituca* and a Pacific Mariner 65 in spiffy condition. The yachts are exposed not only to salt and tropical heat, but also to the uncombusted bunker-oil slag spewed out through the funnels. "The boats can get coated with vile, rusty-looking flakes," says Bruce. "Leave those on the porous gelcoat and they'll permanently stain the deck. Weather permitting, we wash the boats with soap one day, rinse them the next. I also rub down the brightwork with WD-40 to inhibit corrosion." Properly air-conditioning the boats is another task. "Tropical heat can raise interior temperatures enough to delaminate fixtures." After arriving in Fort Lauderdale, he will spend several months skippering *La Pituca* for her Venezuelan owners, Miguel and Sheila Villarreal. He'll do all the route planning and provisioning for a leisurely Caribbean cruise, while teaching the owners to manage the yacht. "Miguel has a Venezuelan captain's licence," says Bruce, "but this West Bay is a new boat for him. Modern yachts are very, very technical. They have space-age programs all demanding their own maintenance schedule."

Born in Toronto, Bruce grew up in a sailing family. His parents met while racing on their families' boats. He spent his summers sailing dinghies at Lake Ontario's east end and started so early in life that he can't recollect when he first set foot on a boat. "I remember being taught racing tactics but not when I learned sailing." After moving west and working in the steel industry, he continued racing and for years lived aboard a classic wooden Chris-Craft on Vancouver's False Creek. Brine was in his blood.

4

That's why, during the 1980 recession when his company wanted to move him to Toronto, he refused. He changed tacks and what had been a "romantic, fun" marine hobby unfurled into a career.

At the invitation of his friend Don Watmough, who was already a charter-boat captain in the Caribbean, Bruce went south to test his options. "Don taught me the basics of how to be, and be seen to be, responsible for other people's yachts. He kicked my butt and was really influential in keeping me focussed. He told me that to create an aura of trust, you're properly dressed at 7:00 A.M. with your lunch in a paper bag. Show them you're ready for work. You can't appear to be out to sea. You don't hang out with rapscallions at the café with a Heineken in your hand. You see, in the tropics, it's easy to slack off. No one works hard so why should you? But I was 42 when I started this career, and though I've put away my share of rum and lobster, I was a bit wiser."

Bruce delivered his first boat in 1982, when "someone needed to have a racing sailboat brought from Florida to St. Thomas." He's sailed, managed and delivered other people's boats ever since. His marine life has included seven years of captaining the 80-foot *Revery*, the last wooden Broward motor yacht built. On this vessel, which cruised the eastern seaboard from Nova Scotia to the Bahamas, he and his crew survived two tropical storms and two hurricanes. He also skippered *Sea Breeze*, an Irwin 52 ketch chartering between New England, Bermuda and the Caribbean. Since then, he has delivered dozens of boats, commanded many corporate yachts and supervised yacht construction. He's earned a U.S. Coast Guard 200-ton master's ticket and a European Community certificate to operate passenger vessels on European inland waterways. He worked at West Bay SonShip Yachts, learning every aspect of the business. During his summer leave, he operated or crewed private and hotel barges on France's canals and rivers — a boatman's holiday. There were dangers, of course. In a 1986 passage on the Irwin 52, the hurricane that sent the *Pride of Baltimore* to the bottom also nailed his vessel. "We were in transit from St. Maarten to Bermuda," Bruce recalls, "when a tropical depression unexpectedly exploded into 90-knot winds. Fortunately I had some of my West

Coast racing buddies aboard this floating condo and they knew instinctively what to do. So we survived."

Has his midlife career makeover fulfilled him? "It's far more work, harder work, to be a successful mariner than anyone can imagine," says Bruce. "Just think what the harsh sea environment does to your workplace. It's constant maintenance just to keep things running." He explains his work consists of more than driving a yacht — it includes weathering gales, traversing locks, repairing engines and electrical systems, troubleshooting, cleaning, provisioning, route planning, arranging for insurance and visas and sometimes putting up with obnoxious guests. He adds that the life of a charter-boat captain may seem romantic, but in reality it's like any corporate job, requiring business planning, accounting, marketing and personnel management. He provides the services the client needs, he notes, which may include organizing catering, tracking expenses, supervising refits and acting as the owner's agent. Yet he has a good measure of independence. "When I signed on with *Revery*, the owner took off on his own boat for three years," Bruce remembers. "His parting shot was: 'Work hard, enjoy and don't call the office for money.'"

Despite the challenges of a sailing career, he loves his life and the thrill of visiting new places, the endless variety of salty bays. He's enjoyed meeting such celebrities as Billy Joel, Christie Brinkley and Jimmy Buffett. He laughingly recalls arms dealer Adnan Khashoggi coming aboard, his every move monitored electronically through an ankle bracelet.

One cost of a travelling marine career, says Bruce, is the difficulty of building and maintaining a relationship. "You're always at work and have no private space. The biggest strain is not having a home base. It's hard when a boat is your only habitat, when you live without a nest." For that reason, he's bought a condo on Vancouver's False Creek, to which he returns as frequently as he can, in part to visit his 95-year-old mother, who always asks him when he's coming home to get a "real job."

Months after delivering *La Pituca* to the Dockwise yacht carrier, Bruce called from his Vancouver condo to report on his latest adventures. "The voyage south was mixed," he said. "We had a great ride down the Pacific coast, running with 30- to 35-knot winds, and the Panama Canal was easy, but we got our asses kicked in the Caribbean. It's a wet ship and it was so rough we could hardly stand up, let alone put a scrub brush to the yachts. When we arrived in Fort Lauderdale, I had to detail the vessel." Bruce skippered the yacht for the next four months, visiting the Bahamas, the Turks and Caicos, and the Dominican Republic and then completing a difficult crossing to Puerto Rico. "The deep water shoals near the Dominican Republic," explained Bruce. "The water always piles up and the waves are intensified by outflow winds from Puerto Rico."

Bruce shared the cooking with Sheila Villarreal. "We swapped recipes. She showed me Argentine methods of cooking meat and other South American dishes. During our meander, there was a coup attempt in Venezuela, an event that made the Villarreals awfully anxious. You see, in that country, 5 percent of the population owns 95 percent of the wealth. Not surprisingly, *La Pituca*'s owners were afraid of nationalization."

The Caribbean trip completed, Bruce was offered a brand-new route: delivering a small Silverton ("only 45 feet") from southern Florida to Decatur, Alabama. "It was a fascinating voyage," he enthuses, "because my mate and I first crossed Florida on the Okeechobee Waterway, transited the Gulf of Mexico and then entered the Tombigbee Waterway near Mobile, Alabama." All these waterways are man-made or superimposed on existing, often wildly meandering rivers. After travelling north on the Black Warrior Canal, going through locks large enough to accommodate commercial traffic, and traversing intriguing marshlands and mangrove swamps, they reached Decatur.

On his next trip, he shepherded a Pacific Mariner 65 from the boat show in Newport, Rhode Island, down the coast for more "boat-show hopping." Bruce and a crew member lived aboard, maintained the boat meticulously and disappeared when the sales team arrived. They delivered the boat to Norwalk in Connecticut for the subsequent boat show, then down the coast to Jersey City, "within sight of Ground Zero." A three-week stint in Annapolis was next. Seven days of hard driving down the Intracoastal Waterway saw the team arrive in Fort Lauderdale.

In his downtime, of which there is little, he cooks ("I'm a gourmet cook"), listens to jazz and blues, and networks looking for new adventures. Now 65, he plans to continue delivering and skippering power yachts as long as he's healthy. The more demanding sailboats, much as he's enjoyed them in the past, are now off the list. "I've grown into a powerboat specialist," he says. He's convinced that, although he's not as quick as a twenty-something, and has less flexible knees, his long experience on the water gives him the edge. "I've been able to position myself so good things happen." He maintains that when yacht owners entrust their huge investment to a skipper, he must exhibit a high level of responsibility. "I know the sea. She's taught me never to underestimate her power. It's the poorly prepared who get into trouble. You have to be ready mentally and physically, because the sea is the most unforgiving element you can imagine. Just because you love her doesn't mean you can disrespect her."

Flo Anderson
life on a rock

Flo Anderson was 37 when she left her commodious Vancouver home for the light station on Lennard Island, a desolate rock near Tofino on Vancouver Island's storm-tossed coast. Her husband, Trevor, had been appointed Lennard's junior lighthouse keeper — his second career after serving 20 years as radio operator and radar fighter controller in the Canadian Air Force. So the intrepid couple downsized their belongings, packed up their four children and boarded the *Camsell*, the Coast Guard icebreaker taking them to their new quarters. It was December 1961, and the weather was icy, windy and ominous.

"Culture shock" is a term used to describe exposure to different customs, usually in a faraway land. Flo moved only about 50 miles, yet the world she entered was as alien as the Congo. Travelling north along the coast toward the godforsaken rock, as Flo wrote later in her autobiography *Lighthouse Chronicles*, "[We saw] a lonely, heavily forested area with deep undergrowth that looked to be inhabited only by light station personnel and a few rustic hermits."

The old house awaiting the family epitomized the word "rustic." Flo believed she'd entered a time warp, returning to a 19th-century pioneer homestead. No furnace. The decrepit wood stove served as both heat source and cooking appliance, with wet, uncut flotsam from the beach the only wood available (they'd naively left the chain saw behind). Winds whistled through the bare, creaky floorboards; water was hand-pumped from the rainwater cistern to an attic tank — it then fed faucets and toilet by gravity; electricity was available eight hours a day, at night when the lighthouse required it. Everything, from supervising the schooling of her brood of four (Garry, 16, Stan, 14, Beth, 12 and Adrienne, 4), to providing food, to washing clothes in the claw-footed bathtub, challenged her grit. Cooking for six, especially feeding two teenaged boys with the nearest grocery store a wild, infrequent sea voyage away, was a trial. Because of variable winds, the stove's damper and thus the temperature were hard to control. Flo's first bread-making efforts spawned little bricks; cakes alchemized into charcoal.

The "hermit" part became equally evident. Because of his duties, Trevor met the senior and other junior lighthouse keepers, but it was weeks before Flo met the other two Lennard Island families. Even 40 years after the event, Flo still vividly recalls the isolation and desolation confronting her. "Writing about Lennard Island was very painful for me," she tells me in her Sidney, B.C., apartment. "These feelings of exile are indelibly imprinted. Life there was traumatic for me. I was so naïve. Recounting it all was therapy. Lots of people have this romantic view of living at a lighthouse. That's why I wrote about it. I wanted people to know what it's really like."

Trevor adds that lighthouse keeping was in a state of flux when he entered the profession. "Unlike the keepers then on station, I'd passed qualifying exams and was thus one of the first 'regular' lighthouse keepers hired by the government. That was the beginning of a change, a very good change. Maybe the training threatened the old guard."

For Trevor, the isolation wasn't as painful and he liked the hard work; it was the people who were troublesome. "The senior lighthouse keeper was an alcoholic misfit with one of the foulest mouths I'd ever heard. He'd run his speedboat into Tofino and return completely inebriated. We'd never experienced that kind of thing before. We'd been in isolated radar stations, but there were groups of people and you could select your friends. On the light station you're forced to live with whoever's there."

Slowly the Andersons improved their lives. They cleaned and painted. Flo unravelled sweaters and used the wool to knit warm socks. She learned to manage the balky stove, baking 26 loaves of bread a week. Trevor asked for the midnight shift and the family adopted the same schedule. They'd go to bed just after lunch and rise for breakfast at 11:00 P.M. While Trevor ran the lights, the kids completed their lessons and Flo freely used the electrical appliances powered by the generator feeding the lights. No distractions. The mornings were devoted to exploring the 18-acre island, slashing paths through the dense salal, investigating tidal pools, cutting wood and building a garden to supplement the meagre pay — $180 a month after deductions.

The family began easing into its rock-bound existence and took pleasure in the warmer summer days with their birds and flowers. Logs were piled up, then split so Flo would have dry firewood to cook meals.

Then calamity struck.

The Department of Transport informed Trevor he was fired. The noxious senior keeper had written a batch of letters reporting that Trevor performed his duties badly and was wrecking the island. "The bottom fell out of our world," says Flo. "To have worked so hard, put up with the isolation, the rudeness and the primitive conditions. It was more than I could bear."

Unwilling to stay on Lennard, Flo took her children and went to visit friends in the Tofino area, while Trevor journeyed to Victoria to protest his dismissal. After a lengthy investigation, with the family returning to Lennard, he was reinstated. Fortunately, in June 1963, he was promoted and appointed senior keeper at Barrett Rock, seven miles outside Prince Rupert in northern British Columbia. The family moved to a more comfortable house this time, although its cistern was empty and the rain, normally plentiful on the raincoast, took a break. Trevor was sometimes sent as relief lighthouse keeper to other stations and, during his absence, Flo ran the lights. "All the wives were part-time lighthouse keepers," she explains. "Unpaid of course. It was just expected. When the man was away, the wife filled the gap."

Trevor and Flo became rock hoppers and seasoned movers. Just four months after settling at Barrett Rock, they were transferred to McInnes Island in Milbanke Sound, midway between Vancouver Island and Prince Rupert. McInnes was just a blip of a mountain jutting up into the sea. Their posting lasted 14 months. Green Island, then the northernmost staffed lighthouse in Canada, was next. Because of fierce winter storms, the valiant family was obliged to wait nearly a week just to go ashore. Flo, calling this latest home an igloo, remembers writing Christmas cards with a hot-water bottle on her lap. The incessant tempests created rotund — and treacherous — ice pillows on the beaches. The Andersons lived through two ice-sprayed winters and then, in July 1966, were transferred to Race Rocks, which became their true home. They stayed 16 years.

Race Rocks, a group of jagged islets lying eight miles from Victoria, is the southernmost point on the Canadian Pacific coast. It is named after the passage separating it from Vancouver Island, which has a tidal race reaching 10 knots. When strong tides and winds oppose each other, standing waves can reach 15 feet. Trevor and Flo, now hardened lighthouse keepers, lived on the largest of the islets and enjoyed the abundant seals, sea lions, whales and birds that colonize the other rocks. They also worked in tandem with nearby Pearson College of the Pacific, whose international students actively study the islets' unique ecology. Captivated by the kaleidoscopic colours and ocean turbulence, Flo began painting seascapes.

In 1974, the couple embarked on a new construction project — the building of their future home, a 44-foot wooden ketch (with an overall length of 57 feet), *WaWa the Wayward Goose* (*wawa* is the word for Canada goose in Ojibway). Flo still laughs about getting a copy of *Chapelle's Boatbuilding* and having to study a new language — marine terminology. Trevor lofted the boat, and over the next eight years they worked a bit each day, with the sailboat slowly taking shape. Getting wood, spruce spars and parts to the lighthouse was a challenge, but with characteristic stick-to-itness, the pair persevered. In 1982, when they retired, *WaWa* skidded down greased rails into the ever-turbulent Race Passage.

"After circumnavigating Vancouver Island in 1983, we realized that life on the lights had thoroughly prepared us for living on a boat," says Flo. "There are so many similarities. At the lighthouse, we did hard physical labour every day and we were in good shape. Because all goods and supplies have to be delivered by boat, we'd learned to do without. There's similar provisioning. Conserving water. The need to prepare. Counting on each other as a couple." They called Pearson College their "home port," then spent time exploring Puget Sound, learning to use a sextant and to cook on a boat's diesel stove.

Flo was adamant that living on a boat should not include being tied to a dock. So they anchored out. They avoided moorage fees. No alcohol. No smoking. No fancy dinners out. They made do so they could afford to immerse themselves in the sinuous complexity of the West Coast. Then, in 1985, they set sail for Hawaii, thinking they might sail around the world.

Much later, after arriving in New Zealand, they decided against circling the globe. "We thought Europe too crowded and everywhere we considered going seemed to have pots of political problems," says Flo. So, slowly, they wended their way home, stopping in Fiji, Pango Pango, Western Samoa and then Fanning Island, with its "magic lagoon and flocks of rays," arriving in Hawaii in late fall. Flo remembered how her celestial-navigation instructor had stated emphatically, "Any fool who crosses the North Pacific in the wintertime deserves what he gets," so they awaited summer in Honolulu.

But sailing north in summer doesn't guarantee an easy passage. When they left in July 1987, an initial calm forced them to motor. Then the Pacific turned unpacific, and a five-day gale drove them within 500 miles of the Oregon coast. The fierce winds ripped the seams on their sails — they had been sewn with thread containing cotton, which disintegrates in the hot tropical sun. Next the engine stopped — they'd run out of fuel. They feared another big wind would drive them onto Oregon's rocky coast.

Flo wryly recalls her depression while standing watch at 5:00 A.M. "Suddenly," she chuckles, "this cheery voice came over the VHF radio and said, 'Hello there, sailboat. Where are you going?'

It was an Alaskan fishing boat en route to Portland, Oregon. Eventually, I summoned up the courage to ask them for fuel. They were pleased to help and we floated jerry cans with some greenbacks attached over to the vessel. Forty gallons of diesel! The ship was called *Dawn*, but I renamed her *Angel of Dawn*. Their kindness allowed us to power all the way into Victoria."

After returning to their home port in 1987, the Andersons continued to live on *WaWa* for the next eight years, indulging in a cell phone the last year aboard. Then they sold the vessel and moved ashore and, at the age of 70, Flo started her lighthouse memoirs. Initially, she intended her musings to serve only as a record for her children. "But," she says, eyes twinkling, "each person reading the manuscript told me to publish it, so I phoned Howard White at Harbour Publishing. Many people think living on an isolated rock is such fun. It's hard, ceaseless work. A routine that doesn't bend. It's been my passion to let others know what life on the lights was really like. Since the book came out, many lighthouse keepers have contacted me to say it was their story too."

Flo and Trevor remain terribly busy. They're new great-grand-parents. They continue the lifelong conversation they've had for more than 60 years of marriage. "We have so many projects," says Flo, "our lives are full. Trevor is writing his own memoirs, pecking away two fingers at the time. Not for publication, mind you. He's just telling his children about the 55 World War II missions he flew out of North Africa."

What advice does this duo have for other intrepid couples? "Our lives taught us to expect the unexpected," concludes Flo. "On the lights and during our Pacific voyage we were, of course, always surrounded by the sea. We appreciate the sea but know it's totally unforgiving. We don't control it. It's powerful. On Green Island the sea catapulted huge logs over the rocks. All this teaches you to be prepared for anything. So when our genoa's clew shackle flogged off, the main blew out and we ran out of fuel, we had to be inventive. Learn to adapt."

"Yep," adds Trevor. "Flo's right. Murphy's law has complete control."

Brion Toss
seven ways to tie a bowline

The afternoon I am to meet Brion Toss in his Port Townsend waterfront rigging shop, he's just scooted outside to Hudson Point Marina to finish installing a genoa on a 60-foot Hawaii-registered yacht. Because he specializes in rigging cruising sailboats for offshore voyages, the owners have requested a thorough inspection before recrossing the Pacific Ocean. I wander down the dock and watch as Brion and apprentice rigger Margie McDonald hoist the sail. "Haul away," he yells. With Brion almost lovingly handling the tough, stiff Dacron fabric, he tutors Margie and the owners on how to furl the huge sail neatly and tightly, each time repeating his clearly stated explanations. "Be sure this line is always taut," he says pointing to a multicoloured strand, "or it won't furl right. Tension is crucial."

The 51-year-old Brion looks like a rigger: compact, almost stocky, strong enough to hoist himself up the mast without help. To stay that way, he attends aikido classes, working toward a black belt. Brown-eyed and ruddy, with silver-touched dark curly hair and the neatly trimmed beard of an old salt, Brion is highly focussed on his craft. He's been rigging for two-and-a-half decades, has produced 10 videos on the subject, written rigging books, invented rigging tools and written numerous articles on the intricacies of rigging. He calls his trade "a huge and broad-spectrum art."

Brion did not grow up to be a rigger. Born in Ashland, Kentucky, he is the son of a secretary and a radio announcer. The family moved as often as new radio stations beckoned, finally settling in the Puget Sound area. In his late teens, career goals vague, Brion leafed through the *Whole Earth Catalog*, the 1968 publication that became the youth movement's bible and unofficial counter culture handbook. Inside the catalogue, a guide to urban survival demonstrated two knots — a sheet bend and a square knot. They were recommended for use, says Brion, "in case you had to get out of a flaming apartment building or escape during a riot." Intrigued, the 17-year-old taught himself the two knots and showed off this newly learned skill to his friend Bart, who'd grown up sailing on a Kettenberg ketch in San Diego. Bart, says Brion, "reached over his right shoulder, I can still see it," and handed over the *Encyclopedia of Fancy Knots and Rope*. "It was a big, dense, horrible book filled with murky black-and-white photographs and only minimal descriptions. I remember opening it — I get shivers just thinking about it — it was an Alice and the rabbit hole feeling."

Brion "descended into the book" and spent most of his time tying knots. That Christmas, his family ("God bless 'em") gave him the much more useful *Ashley's Book of Knots* (first published in 1944 by Clifford W. Ashley), with its 3,854 samples. Brion tied them all. "I remember taking the bus downtown and getting my first spool of manila rope. Six hundred feet of three-eighth-inch rope. 'How will I ever use all that up?' I wondered." But while taking years learning to loop, hitch, lash, braid, plait, splice, intertwine and weave bits of string and rope, Brion discovered he could do more with knots than tie them. "I grew fascinated with the knots' structure, variety and combinations. There are, for example, seven different ways to tie a bowline. It became clear that knots aren't just arbitrary constructions, but tools, profound tools, not like a hammer or crescent wrench — you can't go down to Sears and buy a bowline — but a tool that lives in your hands and in your head. Eventually in your synapses."

During this late 1960s era, filled with revolution, Vietnam War protests, pot and free love, a semi-hippie Brion ("I may have had long hair and lived in communes, but I found the politics odd, brash and self-indulgent") hitchhiked around the United States.

He spent all his time making knots. Thinking that creating income with his art would be useful, he began selling his fancy work — turkheads, key chains, door mats — at street fairs. It provided him "a marginal living, if you don't count the hours and live cheaply." His lifestyle also led him to take part in building sound stages for the music festivals that sprang up almost spontaneously. "I thought music for people was a good idea, and building stages was a lot of fun. I loved running a crew and making things happen literally overnight. It was my first rigging work." It also gave him the first, almost fatal, taste of the dangers of rigging.

"I was on a 45-foot, badly proportioned, narrow tower. After the concert was over, we started to remove the guy wires to drop the tower. A piece of wire tied to the wrong frame pulled the tower over. The whole thing was ridiculously dangerous. For me, this was both 'Engineering 101' and 'Death 101.'" Brion was lucky. He "only" broke an ankle and a knee, although he feels the after-effects in those joints to this day.

Slowly he began to intuit that "all these knots I was studying" almost always serve as part of a larger system, a system that deals with the delivery and resolution of tension and compression: rigging. "Knots, in all their glorious variety, are the connection nodes in the system, and, far from being arbitrary complications, are often highly evolved tools, beautifully suited to specific jobs."

Wooden-boat shows in Seattle and Port Townsend electrified Brion. He "sat at the knee" of Nick Benton who, says Brion, was a protean, Mozart-like rigger, a prodigy of manual and technical skill. Nick died young, like Mozart, but not before inspiring a new generation of riggers to see their work as something more than just "holding up masts and sails." Nick taught Brion the cardinal rule of rigging: *fair leads*, an oft-repeated instruction. "The deeper idea behind this concept," explains Brion, "is that rigging entails the resolution of forces. The smoother and more efficiently we can move those forces about, the better the rigging."

He began learning about loads, the characteristics of the materials used to handle those loads, the blocks, tangs, masts and other hardware that form part of the system. Eventually he

17

came to specialize in what he calls the "densely elegant architecture of sailing rigs," both traditional and contemporary.

Brion believes the traditional craft of rigging continues to inspire the contemporary, in spite of the revolution in rigging materials. It took tens of thousands of years of development to get from a simple manila sheet to the square-rigged ship of the middle 1800s. Then Cornish coal miners discovered that rope (unlike nautical purists, Brion allows the use of the word "rope" in the marine lexicon) could be made out of wire, and within a few years the entire world converted from rope rigging to iron wire, then to steel wire. Sometime in the 1940s nylon and Dacron were invented, making ropes twice as strong for the same diameter, rot resistant, more durable and thus safer than natural fibres. These were followed by high-modulus ropes — Spectra and Kevlar — at least twice as strong as Dacron and far less elastic. From a historical view, the changes in rigging that have occurred in the past 50 years equal all the development heretofore. "Yet, ironically," says Brion, "the traditional skills and knowledge become increasingly more valuable during this rapid flux because that's where the information on the basic principles resides. So a traditionally trained sailor is more valuable than a contemporarily trained sailor because they are more resourceful and have a more intuitive grasp of the nature of the loads. Those things don't change."

Brion opened his first rigging loft in Anacortes in 1978, renting an unused ballroom in the city hall. "It was a scam of a lifetime. A 95- by 55-foot room with bathrooms, showers and gas heat for $150 a month." He laughingly recalls ignoring the business aspects of his enterprise, thinking of them as an inconvenience, an ugly necessity he had to endure to find rigging work. As a result, he was dismally poor without even realizing why. "I didn't want to do office work, you know. I was a RIGGER!"

His personal life changed when he met a sailmaker and moved to Brooklin, Maine, to marry her. But, as Brion puts it, "the marriage was not the most appropriate response, so we got divorced." In Brooklin, home of the WoodenBoat School, he was exposed to many traditional sailing crafts. Putting together the many rigging principles and "nifty wrinkles" he'd learned, he wrote *The Rigger's Apprentice* in 1984. Subsequently, he travelled to Texas to work on an iron barque, the square-rigged *Elissa*. In 1985, he signed up for a six-month stretch as the rigger aboard *Sea Cloud*, a 300-foot, four-masted barque, with 10-and-a-half miles of rope rigging. After joining the ship in Greece, he crossed the Atlantic, gaining his first offshore experience.

In 1986, he returned to the Northwest and chose Port Townsend as the place for his rigging business. This time, he appreciated it *was* a business. "If we fail to care for our business as if it were a living creature, as in fact it is, we won't have the fun of providing our clients with the services. Tracking costs, getting efficient, finding good suppliers and building relationships with clients — those things make it a good business. That was a huge discovery for me, and I've also been blessed with my staff, and with my [second] wife Christian, whose ideas make things happen."

Believing it's his mission to teach, he branched out into videos and workshops. "I've always been evangelical about rigging. It's this wonderful art, which has been grossly misunderstood." He explains it's difficult to overstate how much a lack of information leads to bad rigging, and most of his work is created by other people's mistakes. He argues that on poorly rigged boats, things wear out, or wear out sooner, or make boats less efficient and more dangerous because sailors wear themselves out sooner. "Often, boats are rigged with a plethora of systems. Yet the fundamentals of rigging are pretty direct."

During a workshop in San Diego, while explaining the fundamentals of rig design, he mentioned that cruising sailors are frequently advised to make their rig one size bigger for offshore voyages. "Yet few people will make their propeller a size bigger or the head a size bigger. I tell them it's usually a mistake because often the rig's already one size bigger than it needs to be. Then another increase in size. All this generates extra weight and windage and compression and tension on the hull, because, of course, the heavier wire needs more tension. A woman in the front row slid lower and lower into her seat. She had just equipped

19

her offshore boat with a heavier rig, and so had the previous owner, and the original rigging wasn't small to start with, so she now had this huge heavy rig — all installed with the willing aid and encouragement of the local riggers, to whom it had never occurred to run the ancient load calculations."

According to Brion, rigging in general, and yacht rigging in particular, is the least regulated and least certified craft. All anyone has to say is, "I am a rigger," and that is enough. What Brion hopes for is a certification program verifying that riggers have successfully completed a series of splices; can gauge the destruction test averages for these splices; have passed a course on how to drill, tap and isolate fasteners; and know how to calculate loads on various sorts of standing and running rigging.

How can sailors keep up with all the new rigging materials? "I believe anyone interested in sailing is intelligent enough to step back from the edge and let the racers make the mistakes, break the gear and perform the initial destruction test engineering. Remember, the Cunningham and roller-bearing blocks were tremendously exotic just a few years ago. Now they've been tested and we can all make use of them."

But that doesn't mean sailors should be uninformed. When I ask him about the yankee on our cutter, *Starkindred*, he rattles off a volley of questions. "What kind of halyard do you use? Do you sheet to the same point or is it on a track? Where is it relative to the boat's centreline? Is it straight, on a curve or at an angle to the boat? If so, why? Will the boat notice it if it's wrong? Is the hull shape capable of supporting a more efficient lead, or a more efficient halyard? If not, how do you know? Is that poorly halyarded or sheeted sail affecting your helm?" I realize I have lots more to learn about rigging. "You must remember, rigging extends past the tangs and chain plates," continues Brion, full of passion. "The entire hull is a member of the rigging system. It absorbs the power of the sails and transforms that power into vessel motion."

Brion continues to develop his craft. He's studied the "miraculous" new ropes and found their durability and rigidity is offset by the fact that they break more easily when knotted. He's worked with theatre riggers, arborists, SWAT teams, architects and the U.S. Forest Service. His rigging principles have helped build log structures in the woods and aided mountaineers, rescue workers and firefighters. He's planning to write more books (*The Rigger's Locker* was published in 1992), prepare more videos and teach more workshops so that people can grasp rigging fundamentals regardless of their learning styles. He feels he's continuing to learn himself, every day, from nearly everyone he meets. He's still going aloft on sailboats and counts on continuing climbing masts for at least another decade. "I hope to blossom in the next five years. Harvard prof Wendell Barrett once said, 'The acquisition of knowledge always entails the revelation of ignorance.' I'm convinced we must keep looking for more knowledge. Yet, whatever you're looking for in life, don't ever find it. People who find 'the answer' stop looking, grow complacent, lose curiosity. Their views solidify. And conflict with others who've also found the answer. So I say, 'Keep looking. Just don't succeed.'"

Martin Higgs
the ship handler

Martin Higgs' workshop is enormous. Located in a separate building outside his home in Lantzville on Vancouver Island's east coast, its walls are bedecked with tools and artifacts of every description: curved logging saws, marine ornaments, and rows and rows of photographs of old ships, tugs, ferries and schooners. Outside, a king-size, white-painted ship's bell hangs from a frame; a five-foot-diameter, well-polished propeller embellishes the yard. Here lives a man who loves seafaring.

Martin has marine history in his genes. Born in Nanaimo in 1929, he grew up on tugs. His father was a lifelong captain who, with his brother Billy, ran a tugboat company. "My brothers and I all came up on the tugs," says Martin, a retired B.C. marine pilot, in his gravelly, Satchmo voice. "We berthed ships in Nanaimo, looked after the coal scows." From the time he could walk, Martin spent his time on boats. In fact, anything that got in the way was a nuisance, including school. "The boat was important and our job on the boat was important. School was not." Not faring well in the Nanaimo school system, Martin was sent to Qualicum School for Boys for a few years, but it turned out "those teachers weren't very smart either." So he quit school and became a mate on one of the family's tugs, until his father pressured him into starting his apprenticeship to become a master mariner.

At the age of 17, Martin signed on for a four-year training stint with the Silver Line, a deepwater steamship company. "Silver

Line ran 450-foot, 10,000-ton tramp ships, a bit like the merchant marine, all built alike like the Liberty ships, carrying lumber and general cargo down the American coast." From San Pedro in southern California, Martin's ship, the *Manx*, made for Manila, carrying one of Martin's favourite commodities. "We brought cases and cases of beer. The Filipinos had good beer, but it was right after the war and the Japanese had wiped out most of their breweries. We loved carrying that cargo and I was the one responsible for tallying the stuff. A bit of the fox in the henhouse."

He fondly remembers his time aboard the *Manx*, including meeting "the girl of my dreams in Manila" and leaving her behind as young sailors do, learning splicing and flag signalling, standing watch, scraping rust and serving as quartermaster. Navigation was somewhat dicier. "We had to take a sight every Sunday. The first time I plotted the ship's position we were running up the coast of India and I placed us close to Mount Everest in the Himalayas. The captain came up to me and said, 'You ain't going to make it, son.'"

But as happens regularly in the marine transport business, Martin's ship was sold and his apprenticeship cancelled. He could have joined a British ship at "two pounds, 10 pence" a month, but after earning $48 a month on the *Manx*, he opted to return to British Columbia "to earn a bit of money." He rejoined his father's firm and, after obtaining a temporary skipper's licence, took the helm of a 50-foot tug. In 1953, he earned his master's ticket allowing him to run any size tug from "Vancouver Island to Panama to Halifax." He was just 24.

Martin laughs when he tells me that tugboat captains, whose work concentrated heavily on towing logs, were jokingly called "pike pole navigators" after the poles used to boom logs. "Those are guys who avoid going aground by pushing the pole down and if it's deep enough, then just keep 'er going." He explains that log booming has changed since the 1950s. In those days, logs were towed in flat rafts, not bundled and tied the way they are today. "We had individual logs just sitting there with a swifter over the top. In a storm, they'd break up like kindling wood. You always had to be aware of the weather and the tides."

Some of his work was unusual. In the early 1960s, Martin's tug served as background in several films made on the B.C. coast. Thus he met Rita Tushingham and Peter Finch, stars of *The Girl with the Green Eyes*. He skippered the historic steam tug *Master*, with her faked paddle wheels, for *The Trap* with Oliver Reed. "They put toques on us extras and we became Frenchies from Qweebek." Martin was also the featured tugboat captain in a tale about the breed published in the *Toronto Star*'s *Weekly Magazine*. The accompanying photos show a good-looking, strong man in his early 30s, bare-chested, with a mane of curly black hair, woolly beard, burning cigarette in hand, waiting for a drink.

But films were the exception in the skipper's life. Typically, Martin towed logs through the Gulf Islands, from Silva Bay to Chemainus, to the mainland, up to Seymour Narrows and Cape Caution, down to Victoria. He recalls many wintry southeasterly blows and the unpredictable outflow winds between islands that could dash apart booms in an instant. Along the way he founded his own firm, Tiger Tugs, married, and after becoming father to a son, moved to Gibsons on the Sunshine Coast.

With an old friend, Joe Smith, he started another tug company, JoeMar Marine (named after Joe's wife, Joyce, and Martin's wife, Margaret), operating and chartering tugs. But as the company grew, so did the responsibilities. With up to 25 employees clamouring for a paycheque, Martin was driven to find work for them. Like many small business owners, he struggled to maintain cash flow. "I had some dozer boats, you know, the little tugs that stow the logs, push the bundles and make up the booms. The guys running them were always asking me, 'Where do I go for work?' and 'When do I get my money?'" Martin had turned into an administrator with two phone lines into his house and radiophones on the boats, always worried about meeting payroll.

Even today he remains annoyed by the way the logging companies delayed paying for booms delivered. "'We're up to date,' they'd say. 'The scale to count out board feet isn't here yet.' So I'd ask the bookkeeper, Lucille, if there was any money in the till. She'd cut me a cheque for $2,000 when I was owed five times that amount. They forced us into being a bank for them. Whether they paid me or not, I still had to pay the crew, and Revenue Canada always wanted the withholding taxes right on time."

At the time, two of Martin's brothers had already qualified as marine pilots on the B.C. coast. "I saw my brothers walking around with a so-called intelligent look on their face and a shiny patch on the ass of their pants [that's the way tugboaters talk about pilots; they have a soft job and sit on their butts], and said to myself, 'My brothers are walking around in suits and I'm still with these tugs ... '"

Martin studied for the pilotage exam, which requires intimate knowledge of the B.C. coast up to Alaska. Recognizing that the tug business kept him off the main shipping routes and that working out of Gibsons was too circumscribed, he went back to sea, skippering the *Pacific Challenge*, a large coastal tug towing loads from the Queen Charlottes south and from Texada to Portland. Having thus refreshed his knowledge of the coast, he wrote the pilotage exam in 1974 and, after passing, began another apprenticeship — six months of accompanying established pilots.

British Columbia has a longer coastline than any other Canadian maritime province: 10,557 miles, or roughly three times the width of Canada at its widest. Because of Pacific Ocean gales and storms, heavy fogs, and strong tides and currents coursing through hundreds of narrow waterways, many a ship has foundered on this coast. That's why, since 1875, any foreign-registered ship exceeding 350 tons must by law take a pilot aboard. BC Coast Pilots Ltd. provides the service under contract to Pacific Pilotage Authority, a crown corporation. Most countries require pilots with local knowledge to bring ships in and out of harbour. With good reason. Today's freighters, usually measuring at least 600 feet, not only transport millions of dollars worth of cargo, but also, when leaving the coast for Panama or Hong Kong, carry between 550 and 1,650 tons of bunker oil. "Imagine that oil spill in the Gulf or San Juan islands," says Martin.

He loved being a pilot from the first day. He sold his two companies and moved to Vancouver, his home base for the next decade. What he liked most was the early morning juggling of ships at the quays. Bringing to bear all the experience he had gained handling log booms on the tugs, he'd shift the behemoths around the harbour. "We'd go out at around five or six in the morning and move the ships from one grain dock to another, loading from, say, the Alberta Wheat Pool, and then on to the next grain dock. With each freighter, we'd use two berthing tugs. I knew all the guys; they were artists. I was the head; they were the arms. Together we handled a lot of bulk carriers and container ships in restricted areas, sometimes turning them stern first and then back. It was such a challenge to jockey these ships into position with the tides and all."

Martin calls piloting ships "a piece of cake. You have a ship alongside the dock, two anchors, two berthing tugs and the radio. What can go wrong?" Apparently, quite a few things. Martin recalls one storm-battered ship that came in from the Pacific with its bridge washed out and radio and gyrocompass dead. The Coast Guard told the ship to anchor in Juan de Fuca Strait and await repairs. Martin went aboard to evaluate the situation. With his characteristic can-do approach, he overrode the Coast Guard. "It was three days before Christmas, these guys had no more grub, they were hungry. I judged the ship, the weather conditions and took it home through Active Pass (we rarely pass freighters through there anymore). Today, regulations would start the helicopters flying and they'd have to make repairs before coming in."

Once, on a midnight run from Vancouver to Seattle, Martin saved an American packet with 90 passengers aboard. Close to Turn Point, the vessel's power suddenly died, leaving the steering stuck 10° to starboard. The engineer had accidentally blown both circuit-breaker boards. The ship had no mechanical backups, nor did anyone aboard know the location of the emergency steering. "The captain was a wild, west-coast guy from Seattle who said, 'What the hell are we going to do?' I told him to look after the passengers." But Martin had seen a tug and knew the captain, Bono. He radioed his old friend and, although the tug was pulling a barge filled with highly flammable airplane kerosene, Bono took the ship in tow until a large Vancouver tugboat arrived and hauled the stricken ship to harbour. What if there'd been no buddy tug? "We would have drifted toward the beach and dropped the anchor."

A year before Martin retired, he fell off a rope ladder while descending from a Filipino freighter one cold April night. "Boarding a ship on a rope ladder is the most hazardous part of a pilot's life. It was 10 o'clock, we had a full southwesterly gale in the Juan de Fuca Strait off Victoria, and when the pilot boat came to collect me, the big ship had to make a lee." Martin was in a hurry and although he'd "been down that ladder a thousand times," the leaping waves bounced the rungs off the big ship. Martin couldn't hold on. As he hit the water, his life vest inflated. "But," says Martin, "Mr. Wiseguy me, I hadn't fastened the strap between my legs, because if I meet some gal, I wouldn't want this strap pulled up the crack of my ass. But that blown-up jacket was just about over my head and I couldn't reach the strobe light. I was invisible."

Martin thought he "was a goner" until the deck hand threw a lighted life ring. Eventually, Martin, unable to outswim the swells, floated to the ship's stern where the weatherside wind tossed him on a collision course with the life ring. After being hauled onto the pilot boat, Martin arrived on shore, where an ambulance transported him to a Victoria emergency room, but left him at the door when another crisis called the paramedics away. "I checked in with the nurse. She says for me to wait a minute. Half an hour goes by and I'm sitting there, soaking wet, and so I goes back to the gal and says, 'Any chance of having a shower with you, sweetheart? I'm getting a little cold here.' She sent me home to take a shower, apparently the worst thing you can do for hypothermia. What a mix-up!"

Martin estimates he's piloted more than 5,000 ships and believes his two decades of piloting were among the best for the profession. "Before all these rules, regulations and electronics. I foresee the day computers will replace the pilots. Or politics will." He grumbles about Vancouver's Traffic Services, remarking that once, the freighter's captain and the pilot would competently bring in the ship. "But today," says Martin, "they have two guys from Three Rivers, Qweebek, talking French. You have to drive

a ship according to what they say on shore, not on the water."
He fondly remembers the days before political correctness when
he still got "eyeball exercise from underneath the docks because
the girls all wore skirts"; when cigarettes didn't cause throat cancer or heart disease (he gave up his lifelong fondness for tobacco
and whisky after his cancer and bypass operations); when real
men handled tugs; before "most of the seamen turned out to be
gay."

Yet he's content. He goes fishing in a 14-foot, 1926 lifeboat
he's restored. He putters in his workshop and has talked his grand-
son into becoming a ship's engineer because there are always
jobs for "a pig-iron polisher." With a bunch of other mates, he's
created the Ancient Mariners, who meet for a monthly lunch in
Nanaimo, "a fellowship thing, you know, just a bunch of old
bullshitters talking." He collects marine charts dating back to
1819, knows where the B.C. shipwrecks are, hunts for old pictures of tugs. "I've had a good life, but like my wife says, it's been
boats and tugs. I've never thought of anything else."

He and three other guys are supposed to go to Prince Rupert
to get a 61-foot tug and take turns skippering it to Vancouver.
"We'll be hot bunking all the way. I'm itching to go. When they
called and asked me, I told 'em, 'I'm coming. Right now.'"

Keith Sternberg
messing about with machines

P_utt-putt! Putt-putt! Putt-putt!_ The motor on Keith Sternberg's _Aeolus_ beats a tattoo across Shoal Bay on Lopez Island on its way to visit us on _Starkindred_. A Volvo Penta MD2B propels his 1939 wooden Norwegian pilot boat, designed by Colin Archer. The engine is one of Keith's more modern possessions; he guesses it was installed about 1970. "Rather new machinery for me," he says with a chuckle. I climb aboard and look over his classic yacht. He cautions me about touching the newly tarred lifelines. The wooden blocks are hand-carved _lignum vitae_ ("wood of life" in English), a tropical hardwood. Everything is neatly painted, but the interior of the narrow 26-footer is rustic. A pile of firewood sticks is stacked under the two-burner cast-iron stove, which heats the vessel and serves as cooker. Rough bunks with grey wool blankets line the boat's flanks. No GPS in sight. With its 5.5-foot draft and 13,000-pound displacement, I don't expect this boat to be a slippery sailer. And that's just fine with Keith. "For me," he says candidly, "it's character first, sailing ability next and comfort last. I enjoy the feel and weight of her."

Keith earns his living as a compass adjuster (he cautions me not to call him a "compass swinger") and services mostly tankers because they are required by law to have their compasses corrected annually. "Although most ships now steer by gyro and electronic navigational equipment, I still like an old-fashioned compass. And it's important they're properly adjusted. I just worked on a tanker whose compass had been corrected after some welding work in Singapore. But someone messed up — it was off between 40 and 50 degrees. Can you imagine, with all that oil aboard?" Keith calls himself a traditionalist, and his interests lie in machinery and instruments — the older, the better.

After we putt-putt to the dock, we drive to his Lopez Island farmhouse, where he gives me a tour of his workshop. The horizontally pine-planked walls are covered with antique timepieces and ships' clocks, chronometers, brass pressure gauges and a time signal from a Fort Collins government station. He also shows me an engraved 1880 London Polaris compass he's used for 35 years, and an Azimuth computer invented by a World War II naval captain. A large belt-head lathe with multiple leather straps dominates nearly half the shop and, he explains, allows him to machine parts for engines, create the tiniest screws and bolts, and polish clocks' pivots. He tests and repairs steam gauges for the many ships that still use them. He's made a wooden replica of a backstaff (a precursor to the sextant), a navigational device that replaced the astrolabe and cross staff. He also likes old pocket watches and uses them when adjusting compasses. "They're great," says Keith. "The watch reflects local suntime and I can find the azimuth."

The slim 54-year-old has light brown hair, greying at the temples. He speaks quietly, unassumingly, in his old, dusty, discombobulated house (it's obvious the love of repairing a chronometer outshines his desire to replaster the ripped-out ceiling in the dining room). He and his young wife, Shannon, whom he calls his "child bride," enjoy the Lopez Island lifestyle, with its leisurely pace and the freedom to hop onto his vintage yacht for a friendly sail. "You get used to a place like Lopez," he says. "The mainland is kind of a foreign country."

His "island time" way of life is an acquired taste. Born in Seattle, he joined the Corinthian Yacht Club and the Sea Scouts as a youth, but can't quite recall how that happened. Although his friends liked racing Six Metres, Stars and Dragons, Keith's interests focussed on commercial, square-rigged sailing ships. He'd found Alan Villiers' tomes on old sailing ships in the library, and their adventures stoked his imagination. Although he grew up in the 1960s, he had little interest in hippie culture. "I don't think we had hippies in my school," he says. "Even tobacco and marijuana were things I wasn't much aware of. I was probably a nerd or had my own brand of hippiedom on ships and boats."

At 18, he tramped the waterfront looking for a job, but soon discovered that Villiers' sailing schooners had been replaced. "But the vessels that moved by boiled water intrigued me, so I asked for a job aboard *Virginia V*." That ship, a 122-foot, steam-powered passenger vessel built in 1921, still cruises Puget Sound today. Not needing a deck hand, the captain hired him as a fireman. "It wasn't hard to get the hang of it," says Keith. "The old machinery was low-tech and primitive. The fireman showed me how to fire a boiler, keep the steam pressure at 500 pounds and oil the engine and auxiliaries. There were valves for oil and steam, a chain controlling the damper and a mirror to see if it was smoking. You just adjusted the air and the fuel to keep that fire burning clean. I loved it instantly." The captain was in his 80s, the engineer in his 70s, and they had changed little on the ship over the years, something that suited Keith. "It was like stepping into the past," he recalls. "It didn't even have a telegraph, just a gong and jingle. One clang on the gong was for half ahead, two clangs for half astern, a jingle for full speed ahead, a combined jingle and a bell for dead slow ahead. I could hear the bells while I was handling the fire and knew when we'd need more, or less, steam. A good system, actually."

The Vietnam War was hot and 18-year-olds were being drafted. To avoid that fate, Keith enrolled in oceanography at the University of Washington but continued working on *Virginia V* as well, this time on deck. At 19, combining his Sea Scout and other boating experience, he obtained a 100-ton or "small master's" licence. He worked on *Virginia V* with Captain Albert Smiley, "a good old boy who first went to sea on a four-masted schooner in 1902. He was the real article." As the aging captain lost his eyesight and strength and grew more hesitant around the ship, he relied on Keith to manoeuvre and dock the classic vessel. Keith enjoyed the work and remained on the steamship for several years.

Then Leonard Shrock, who ran Captain's Nautical Supplies, where Keith shopped for charts and nautical instruments, offered Keith a position as apprentice compass adjuster. Shrock had operated a school for compass adjusters during World War II for the U.S. Navy. Keith, wanting to learn something new, signed on. The U.S. government had stopped the draft by then, so Keith left university. "It was useless and they weren't teaching anything I wanted to learn." He was pleased to study the compass adjusting craft, but hated sorting charts and putting price tags on instruments and books. "I'm just not a storekeeper," he says. "It's extremely boring. I was left out on the beach when I really wanted to be out on the water." Thus, in 1972, he took a job on a tugboat bound for Sitka, Alaska.

After commanding the tug and delivering endless loads of gravel for parking-lot paving, he switched to tugs that towed logs for the local pulp mill. He found log-boom towing on the *Martin D* an exciting job. Exciting? "From a distance you see a tug towing logs and it might seem a boring thing," says Keith, still remembering the glory of it. "Sure, you don't go fast. But you don't have good control of these acres of logs. You're at the mercy of the tides and you must avoid bad weather that can spill your tow. So there's tension all the time." He vividly remembers a tow down twisting Surges Narrows, riding the ebb, with rocks everywhere, in the middle of the blackest night, no lights anywhere, with 70 sections of valuable spruce and cedar logs. "The captain was a pro, but this was hard work with a crew of four. Boom chains are heavy, chaining the various rafts together, securing them and later unchaining them, all of it is demanding."

After some time in Alaska, Keith missed Seattle and headed home. Once there, he went to see Churchill Griffith, who owned the Washington Tug and Barge Company and shared Keith's interest in old ships. Having secured a job, Keith began barging fuel oil, gasoline and stove oil all over Puget Sound. He ran the circuit between Port Angeles, Port Townsend and Olympia and shuttled between the refineries in Anacortes and Silverdale, delivering all the gasoline used in Seattle, Bremerton and Gig Harbor. The barge could carry 9,000 barrels of fuel; Keith skippered the tug and a tanker man pumped the fuels into pipes running back to tank farms on the beach. In this manner, they supplied the local service stations. "We delivered fuel to Roche and Friday harbors, and Blakely and Orcas islands." Keith specifically remembers having to go ashore in Port Townsend to hustle the tanker man out of the local tavern, hoping he was sober enough not to pump the fuel into the bay. Fortunately, they never had an accident.

As Keith's marine experience grew, so did his hankering to go into business for himself. On days off, he'd been cruising around in an old steam tug he'd bought. Stopping by to visit a friend one day, he ended up trading his small tug for a larger one, although she had a blown engine. "The *Bee* was a lucky boat for me," says Keith, eyes shining. "The 63-foot wooden boat was built in 1901 but she needed new propulsion. Naturally, I'm thinking of something old-fashioned and I found, very luckily, an excellent direct-reversible Atlas Imperial just the right size for the boat — a 14,000-pounder, 13 feet long."

Keith quit his job at Washington Tug and took six months to put the engine together. He'd been living on a semi-abandoned steamship for several years and knew all the old-time mariners. "My best friends were all over 80," he chuckles. "There was a lot to be learned from those old boys and one of them helped me with the Atlas. In the 1920s he'd worked as a guarantee engineer for the Atlas Imperial Engine Company and knew everything there was to know." With this outside expertise, Keith got the boat running. It was an economical project — Keith had obtained the vessel through a swap and paid only $600 for the engine. "I was close with a dollar," he says with characteristic understatement. He spent money on parts and moorage and lived on the tug while grease monkeying. "I'd married by then and my [first] wife and I lived aboard. It was a very small accommodation — a little fo'c'sle, a tiny captain's cabin, a galley on deck and the rest of her was engine."

For the next five years, Keith towed logs with his 70-year-old tug. He covered the booming grounds up Hood Canal, Lake Washington, Tacoma, Olympia and Shelton. He found the work

interesting, and running his old *Bee* was made even more challenging because he refused to put radar on the boat, despite Puget
Sound's notorious fogs. "I remember one night," Keith reminisces,
"taking a raft out in the Milwaukee Waterway near Tacoma. It
was so foggy that, looking from the pilot house, I couldn't see the
stern and certainly not the 800 feet of logs behind us. But I always kept a detailed logbook and every course was carefully logged
because we had no degrees on the compass either. When the
weather was bad, I'd look in the log to see what worked the last
time. We'd blow the whistle and keep going. No accidents at
all."

Later, after selling the *Bee*, Keith hauled sand and gravel
through Seattle's Ballard Locks with other tugs he bought, and
learned ever more about the Atlas engines propelling them. That
led to his next position. He was hired as an Atlas engineer by the
Foss Company, which owned an old steel-hulled seagoing yacht,
the *Thea Foss*, built in 1929 for silent-movie star John Barrymore.
"It was 125 feet of teakwood-and-brass-and-rivets type of a ship
and Foss bosses would take people out every day and ply them
with drinks. That's how they did business. This archaic boat had
two 75-horse engines, 36,000 pounds apiece. I thought it'd be
for a season or two, but I just loved that old boat. She had engine
room controls but none in the pilot house. There was a telegraph
for each engine, and a big brass lever shooting air to start it. No
direct reversible or clutch. Just me. It was such fun. Had a wrench
in my hand all the time that season." Keith lived aboard in the
summer and worked a 30-day month during cruises. In winter,
the ship sometimes lay idle. Keith stayed 14 years. He eventually
changed the engines from salt-water cooling, which had rotted
and corroded the old cast iron, to fresh-water cooling. It required
hand-machining practically the entire engine. "This wasn't a job
changing parts, like you do in modern machinery," says Keith.
"This was hand-fitting every last bit."

In 1970, Keith and his first wife had bought 75 acres on Lopez,
in part to get away from the pollution of the mills, trains and
docks in Tacoma. Keith grew wheat, raised goats and chick-
ens, and farmed with Belgian dray horses. He found that the

animals, unlike machines, didn't necessarily do what you wanted them to do. For years, he combined his tugboating, Foss duties and farming, but found it daunting to do it all. "One day, thinking about the farm, I realized, 'Hey, I keep doing this and it's not accomplishing anything and I'm not even making any money.'" The tensions contributed to his marriage break-up. During these years, for nostalgic reasons, he'd still visit *Virginia V* and occasionally lend a hand when steam came out of places it shouldn't, so when funds were raised to restore the vintage steamship, Keith got the job of rebuilding the Atlas engine. It took three years to reconstruct the reciprocating steam engine, and Keith enjoyed it immensely. Along the way, he realized he'd become the custodian of half-forgotten ways of doing things. "Now I'm the old-timer. Just as I palled around with those old guys when I was a kid, now people come to me like *Virginia V* people did when they wanted their worn-out engine fixed. Fortunately, I'm only 54."

Keith adjusts about 60 to 70 compasses a year, and his skill in rebuilding vintage engines remains in demand. The rest of the time he puzzles out solutions to the pesky problems of restoring antique chronometers. He's always liked old clocks and tinkered with a few over the years. "I managed to blunder into a fellow who had a collection of precision clocks, chronometers and all the tools it took to build and maintain them. It was like visiting the British Museum. I was able to buy most of his stuff and my shop grew out of his collection." A chronometer, explains Keith, is a specialized kind of horology. "Detents — a tiny part, with springs and a sapphire jewel — are the heart of the chronometer, and in many older chronometers, that's the part that's broken. There's no more tedious job than making a new one. How the old boys did it I don't know, in those dark shops with no tools and no light." He's also working on a formula for resilvering chronometer dials. "It's not a bright shiny silver but a dull white silver. I've found silvering recipes, but I don't think all the information is quite there so I've experimented with making my own, using silver nitrate, salt, cream of tartar and ground-up chalk dust. There's always a challenge to figure something out."

Much as Keith likes the past and its technologies, he tangos just a bit with modernity. E-Bay, with its many esoteric treasures, is a constant lure and he's both bought and sold antique nautical instruments through the website. Considering his use of auctions on the Internet, would he take along a GPS if he were sailing to Tahiti? Keith leans back and ponders. "When Slocum was losing his reckoning on his longitude, he took a lunar sight and crows about it in his book. He made good his landfall and there's something to be said for that. But if the weather's dark and murky, you don't get a sight for two weeks and you're near a lee shore, you have to balance these things out somehow. For myself, I'd better hedge my bets and take a GPS, but I'd hide it in the bilge until I got concerned."

Ken Burton
the patriot on
St. Roch II

Captain Ken Burton (Sergeant, Royal Canadian Mounted Police) sailed from Vancouver on Canada Day, 2000, to circumnavigate North America in a 66-foot aluminum Raven Class patrol catamaran, *St. Roch II*. Skippering the history-making police vessel normally used for coastal patrol in British Columbia, Ken, with a crew of three other officers, retraced the voyage of a famous Canadian Arctic ship, the original *St. Roch*. That ship, a 105-foot Douglas fir-and-ironbark RCMP patrol schooner, had spent decades in the Arctic. Ken's goal? To raise enough funds to save the first *St. Roch*.

The historic ship, built in 1928 by Burrard Dry Dock, was commanded by Captain Henry Larsen and his Mountie "horse sailors," who served the Arctic and its people for more than two decades. Sometimes called the "Viking Mountie," Larsen took local residents to hospital, delivered mail and maintained law and order. In 1940, *St. Roch* set off as part of a secret mission to Greenland to protect the mines producing cryolite, a mineral essential in aluminum smelting for aircraft construction during World War II. Because of unusually cold weather, it took three years for the ship to reach Greenland. Nevertheless, the vessel accomplished a milestone: she was the first to cross the icy region from west to east, and the voyage helped cement Canada's sovereignty in the north. Following that historic feat, *St. Roch* achieved another first: in 1950 she circumnavigated North America. After the schooner returned to Vancouver, she was retired from service and Parks Canada made her the centrepiece of the Vancouver Maritime Museum. But her fortunes waned. Although the ship was named a national historic site, funding was cut, maintenance plummeted and dry rot invaded. Without robust infusions of cash, the ship was fated to moulder into dust.

Ken Burton couldn't let that happen.

In 1998, he received the RCMP's permission to begin fundraising. The timing was right. A host of maritime-history events were in the offing: the Tall Ship Races in North America, the 500th anniversary of Cabot's Newfoundland landing and the world travels of the replica of Captain Cook's *Endeavour*. Moreover, the RCMP was celebrating its 125-year anniversary. "We wanted to bring history alive by repeating *St. Roch*'s circumnavigation of North America, use the voyage as an educational module and, of course, raise money for the old ship's restoration," explains Ken. "Everyone thought the venture was supported by the government. It was not."

In fact, raising funds for the journey proved difficult. When Canadian corporate officers heard about the plan to pilot a thin-skinned aluminum vessel through Arctic ice packs, they backed away. "They argued it couldn't be done," says Ken. "And they feared being associated with failure. Encouragement, yes; money, no." He recalls visiting the Hudson's Bay Company Toronto headquarters to make a pitch for funding from the HBC's educational foundation. An HBC vice-president made it clear he only supported projects that brought customers into the stores. "But," Ken protested, "as an educational foundation, you're getting a huge tax break." The VP told him to get out. Eventually, only Alcan and Trendwest Resorts supported the voyage in a significant way.

Nonetheless, Ken remained determined to succeed. He worked closely with the Vancouver Maritime Museum's executive director, James Delgado, and together, they continued to seek funds. They persuaded the Coast Guard to send the icebreaker *Simon Fraser* from Halifax through the Panama Canal to meet *St. Roch II* in Alaska. Ken convinced some equipment manufacturers that a passage incorporating conditions from the Arctic to the tropics was an unparallelled opportunity to test their equipment's durability. Thus he collected a water maker, dehumidifier, furnace, radar and sonar.

He acquired paint, MAN engine support, Arneson drive systems and Nobeltec electronic charts. Fully provisioned, tanks filled to capacity with 1,100 gallons of diesel, its predecessor's ship's bell aboard, and multiple stops planned for the more than five-and-a-half-month voyage, *St. Roch II* zoomed north. "Just like the days of the old explorers," chuckles Ken. "You know, Amundsen and Frobisher left port just ahead of their creditors."

The catamaran arrived in Tuktoyaktuk on August 4, then sailed to 75°N, just 900 nautical miles from the North Pole. To their amazement, they encountered little ice. "We never needed *Simon Fraser* to plough a path for us," says Ken. "In fact, we never touched ice. If anyone still doubts the climate is changing ... A couple of the crew even went swimming, though I must admit, it was a very short swim."

A tall, stocky man, Ken, born 43 years ago in Orillia, Ontario, didn't set out to be either a modern Northwest Passage explorer or a Mountie. "I was supposed to be a lawyer," he grins. "My dad wanted a doctor, an engineer and a lawyer in the family. He got the first two." Instead, Ken studied art and photography and began his career as a medical photographer. "I worked at Toronto Western Hospital and our equipment was often used by the police forensic team. That's how I got interested in police work. I applied to the RCMP, thinking I'd work in the crime lab. But after attending the training academy in Regina, I ended up in North Vancouver, working in serious crime, surveillance and communications. Never did work in a lab."

Along the way, Ken became a skilled scuba diver and often dove from RCMP boats searching for murder weapons and victims of drowning. "I loved being outdoors and was immensely pleased to join the marine unit," he reveals. "We focus on drug interdiction, immigration and port security." He moved with his wife, Patricia, and their son and daughter to Sechelt on the Sunshine Coast, and worked out of Pender Harbour, patrolling in a 41-foot monohull from Agamemnon Channel and Princess Louisa Inlet to Lasqueti. He also enrolled at the Pacific Marine Training Institute and earned his 350-ton master's ticket, allowing him to navigate 200 miles off the coast — the right ticket to complete the circumnavigation of

North America. "The trip had been talked about for a while," he continues. "And it was a dream of mine to do something like this, something with the potential of making a real difference."

During the Arctic Ocean transit, one of Ken's tasks was to "repatriate" photos taken during the RCMP's long Arctic tenure. Several of the Mounties stationed there had been amateur photographers, and their shots included portraits of the local population. These photos had been scanned and downloaded onto CDs. With moist eyes, Ken recalls how the Inuit viewed pictures of themselves as children, of their parents and other relatives. Few of these northern dwellers owned any images of their ancestors, and the pictorial re-creation of their past was a profoundly emotional experience.

Then local Inuit Louis Kamookak told the *St. Roch II* crew about graves from the doomed Franklin expedition — previously undiscovered graves. "I was very moved that Louie trusted us enough to show us these burial sites on Keeuna," says Ken. After going ashore, they found the remains of five Franklin expedition members who had perished in 1848. Each of the graves had been outlined with stones the size of dinner plates. The mounds were covered with something resembling a fungus, or fibrous mould, but it was wool — the fibres were once sailors' uniforms. Nearby a large fire pit, still containing charcoal, led to questions. What did expedition members burn when no firewood was available? Is this a possible indication of cannibalism? "It was heartbreaking to walk on the ground these explorers had walked," says Ken. "You ask yourself, what would I have done if I'd been in those British sailors' shoes 150 years ago? It was eerie to realize the landscape hadn't changed since then. Those people, desperate and dying, looked at the same scene." Archeological expeditions are planned and may add information about the still-mysterious demise of Sir John Franklin, his crew of 128, and the ships *Erebus* and *Terror*.

Ken recalls one other Arctic adventure. "We awoke one morning and spied an iceberg that had drifted onto our rode and was pushing us ashore. As we jumped up to go on deck, we noticed a hulking polar bear staring at us through the porthole.

We managed to shoo the beast away, but had to cut the rode to release the berg and avoid going aground."

After passing through Davis Strait to the Labrador Sea, *St. Roch II* sped down the east coast of North America, calling on Canadian and U.S. ports. Challenges and joys punctuated the voyage. *St. Roch II*'s crew visited the town of St. Roch, Québec, the town after which the ships are named, received a heroes' welcome in New York and stopped in Fort Lauderdale. In Cuba, the catamaran's sonar array caused the ship to be detained by police. "It took the influence of the Canadian ambassador to get us released from our moorage in Marina Hemingway," says Ken, rolling his eyes. *St. Roch II* trekked on to the Caymans, then was dwarfed by the tanker sharing a lock in the Panama Canal. Turning north, the vessel halted several times in Costa Rica and then whizzed up the Central American west coast toward Mexico.

Their 30-knot speeds caught the attention of the military in Puerto Madero, the first Mexican stop. Suspected of being a drug running ship, *St. Roch II* was boarded on arrival. "A bunch of 16-year-olds pointed rusted M-16s at us. All our paperwork had been sent to the harbour master so we had nothing to show them. Eventually, we were able to convince them we were policemen."

Ken notes that while circumnavigating the continent, he was exposed to a great cross section of people, some extremely wealthy, others exceedingly poor, and sometimes that poverty led to extortionate fees or demands for bribes. By the time Ken arrived in Acapulco, he'd grown tired of demands for money. "There's normally some port fee. But I had a letter from a high official authorizing us to travel in Mexico without paying fees in every port. When we arrived in Acapulco a bunch of guys rushed up to help us moor and demanded $100. I brandished the letter. The port captain got mad. I got tough. Then the Canadian consul arrived and told us two Colombian generals wished to visit the boat — the model might suit their drug-interdiction program. The generals arrived in great style, limos, bodyguards, aides, miles of gold braid. The port captain vanished." But not for good. An 80-foot military ship loaded with 50-calibre machine guns hailed *St. Roch II* when she left the harbour. Ken estimated that the gunship was capable of steaming about 10 knots. He put *St. Roch II* in gear and blasted out of the harbour. After stopping in several more Mexican and American ports, he returned to Vancouver on schedule.

Did the voyage save the old *St. Roch*? Incredibly, it did. After Ken returned, donations flowed in. "Corporations, institutions and governments suddenly gained interest in the project. Success bred success. The City of Vancouver came aboard with sustainable funding. Heritage Canada found money. And corporations showed up cheque in hand. Not huge amounts of money, but a stream big enough to restore and maintain the vessel." Ken credits some of the late donations to the immense amount of publicity the project generated, with full-page stories in *The New York Times, The Montreal Gazette, The Kansas City Star* ("don't ask me why"), papers in Cuba, Japan, the Netherlands and Norway. The daily updated website received at least 2 million hits. Ken estimates the news reached 70 million people.

Looking back on the venture fills Ken with satisfaction. "Everyone kept repeating it couldn't be done," he says. "No thin-skinned aluminum boat could ever go that far and get through the ice, they told me. But with planning, great equipment, and common-sense navigation, an aluminum-hulled vessel can safely navigate the Arctic Ocean and circle the North American continent."

Ken believes *St. Roch II*'s odyssey demonstrates we can still have adventures in the third millennium. "We must capture our dreams, never just be spectators to the world or be afraid. Get out there and push the limits. Explore. There are things to discover. This voyage was much more than a boat trip — it was about life, attitude, discovery, history, tradition, pride. It's been a tremendous honour to follow in the wake of *St. Roch* and Henry Larsen. Canadians have a common shore and there's infinitely more that brings us together than keeps us apart. I tell people who think we lack a Canadian identity to visit Vancouver on Canada Day, see the Arctic and its people's resilience, endure the hard handshake of a Québec miner, and listen to 'Oh Canada' sung in French, English and Inuktitut. I heard children sing it in all three languages."

Carol Hasse
the artist of canvas

The second-floor sail loft is long and narrow. Light streams in from windows on both sides of the building that once served as Port Townsend's U.S. Coast Guard Armory. From these east and west windows, the sailmakers can see not only Hudson Point Marina right outside, but also both the Olympics and Mount Baker. Huge triangular pieces of hefty white Dacron lie flat on the smooth, grey floor, flanked by a row of seven industrial sewing machines. Stainless-steel measuring sticks are scattered about. Shelves and cubbyholes line the walls between the windows, storing sail tapes of all dimensions, shackles, slides, thimbles, leech cleats, fat spools of polyester thread. White spiral hoses loop along walls and ceilings, sucking out any noxious fumes created by the hot knives that cut and seal line, thread and other hydrocarbon products. CDs and music tapes keep people mellow. Staff member Will Moran sits on a bench, hand-sewing a series of grommets into the foot of a sail.

Everything in this cheerful, friendly loft, which houses Carol Hasse's Port Townsend Sails, is designed to create top-quality sails and ensure a happy staff. Hasse, as she's known to legions of friends around the world, founded the loft nearly a quarter century ago, and some of her employees have been with her for 20 years. When the lean, outgoing sailmaker talks about those decades, she looks back in wonder at the convoluted way her career as a quintessential offshore sailmaker evolved.

Hasse, born in 1951, grew up in a non-nautical family in Camas, Washington, a mill town on the Columbia River. "On the river, powerboats were it, windsurfing hadn't been invented and you either water-skied or sat on the beach," she says. As a high school student, she earned good grades which led to a scholarship at the University of Puget Sound. She presumed a university education would go beyond memorizing and taking tests, but found few opportunities for independent learning. She also actively protested the Vietnam War and, full of idealism, searched for traditions outside the military-industrial complex. At 19, after a year at university, she decided to hitchhike around the world to find a place whose politics she could "relate to." She flew to London and spent a year hitching rides through 23 countries.

Unexpectedly, she discovered the truth of what G. K. Chesterton wrote a century ago: "The whole object of travel is not to set foot on foreign land; it is at last to set foot on one's own country as a foreign land." While Hasse backpacked through Europe, she'd assumed the Norwegian fjords and the Black Forest would outshine nature in the Pacific Northwest and was disappointed. She'd imagined Europe's ancient culture would far outclass the ruffians in Seattle. "I'd embraced the ideals of world peace and a non-materialistic lifestyle," she explains. "Instead, I found the European countries caught up in fashion consciousness. I also discovered no other place offered any approximation of gender equity. In Europe, feminism was just in its infancy. I came to appreciate that, maybe, I did belong on the west coast after all."

When Hasse returned home, she visited Dory Brooking, who'd encouraged her to travel. Dory and her husband, Brook, were awaiting the completion of their Cascade 42 and invited Hasse to crew on the yacht. They left in September 1972, with seven people aboard. "It was great," says Hasse enthusiastically. "For these people, it was a family holiday and the more the merrier. But right off Astoria we hit 70-knot winds. It was my first ocean trip and I figured, oh well, this is what it's like, not knowing storms can and should be avoided. Although we put out a sea anchor, we were dragged back 120 miles over a 24-hour period.

Fortunately it was a southeasterly and it blew us offshore rather than onto the rocks. My first sail in hurricane-force winds! After the storm was over, whales spouted, birds swooped. I was hooked."

Hasse sailed with the Brookings to San Francisco, where she joined the Hutchings family (who'd built both the Brookings' and their own Cascade) and harbour-hopped the California and Baja coasts. She taught herself celestial navigation and received further instruction from Mr. Hutchings. When they reached Puerto Vallarta, the Hutchings turned back north, but, says Hasse, "I was totally ready to continue travelling. As I'm rowing across the harbour somebody yells out, 'Hey, we need crew,' and that's how I began crewing on different boats." She boat-hiked to Acapulco, to Costa Rica and then to the Galápagos, where she spent five glorious weeks at a time when few sites were off limits. Her skill as a celestial navigator remained in demand because many boaters had sailed only from harbour to harbour and gunkholed along the coast, thus gaining only meagre navigational experience. Hawaii was next. After flying home from there, she backed and filled while considering her career options. "I liked hiking, sailing and playing my guitar, but I couldn't make a living with those activities. I'd worked summers at the Camas paper mill, and although the money was good, it wasn't a career I coveted. I wanted to stay connected to the water. Perhaps, I thought, being a boat builder was an option."

While visiting some college chums, she found that seven of them had joined together to build a Skookum 47 ketch. Hasse linked up with the group and got the job of making the sails. To learn the basics, she signed up at Schattauer Sails in Seattle and helped sew the ketch's sails while living at Shilshole on a vintage 90-foot tug. Schattauer was a master German sailmaker and had specific, traditional ways of constructing sails, ancient wisdom Hasse incorporates in her own sailmaking to this day. At the end of 18 months, the group launched the boat and sailed to Desolation Sound. "It was just heaven and I discovered that even though I'd been to these places in the South Pacific and Central America, this was as good as it got right here in my own backyard," she says, tucking a lock of shoulder-length hair behind one ear.

Hasse moved to Port Townsend and began a "little varnish business" in a corner of the building which now houses her loft. While living on a gaff-rigged wooden yacht, the *Grey Gull*, which she maintained for friends, she became a leader in establishing the Port Townsend Wooden Boat Festival. Then she was hired by Sail Systems to make some sails, a job that turned into a further two-year apprenticeship. When her boss took his sewing machines and went to sea in 1978, she and a business partner, Nora Petrich, borrowed $5,000, bought new sewing machines and carried on in the loft. Noting the explosive growth in offshore sailing, they focussed on building extra-sturdy sails, with the hand-reinforced details and triple stitching that make sails more durable and maintainable. The business took off.

Marketing grew partly through Hasse's sailing on other people's yachts, a tradition that began in 1980 when she was invited to crew on a friend's boat on a Hawaiian voyage. "But," she chuckles, "the wind was wrong and we dropped anchor in the Marquesas instead, where I met a New Zealand boat whose owners ordered a full set of sails. I measured the boat there, came home, made the sails and shipped them. Since then, I never go anywhere without a 100-foot tape. Pretty much everywhere I've gone I've made a connection and ended up making sails."

Hasse has travelled extensively over the years, sailed on every possible boat — gaff- and square-rigged schooners, sloops, cutters, ketches, yawls — and made sails for all of them, making her name a brand that's instantly recognizable. One day at a boat show, she met John Neal, who teaches offshore cruising seminars. She remembers John looking at her sails and remarking they'd be perfect for offshore voyaging. "Yeah," she answered, "that's what I build them for." Since then, Hasse has participated in John's seminars and numerous other offshore cruising workshops, teaching sail selection and many other topics — an interaction she loves. Along the way, John began teaching offshore cruising on the water and asked Hasse to join in the instruction. "We flew to Raiatea and chartered Peterson 44s. I did that in November and March for about five years. We'd go to from Raiatea to Bora Bora and all those heavenly places, and I grew comfortable and familiar with that part of the world, always growing as a mariner." All this experience on the water allowed her to acquire her 100-ton U.S. Coast Guard master's ticket. Meanwhile, the sail loft was a going concern and the employee base — all women at first, but now including three men — has grown to 12. Hasse's marketing through the sailing seminars was highly effective, and in 1995 she bought out her business partner and made another sea change. She adopted Grayson, now seven, and is teaching him how to sail on *Lorraine,* the 25-foot Danish lapstrake Folkboat she's owned for a couple of decades. "I've stepped back from being a Wooden Boat Foundation board member and focussed on being a mom. What a new dimension that adds to everything!"

Hasse actively pursues sail training for women. "I've found that when women teach women, it is generally more empowering. When it's only women aboard, they can't use the excuse that men know about mechanics, navigation or sail shape because of their testosterone. Women alone learn they don't have to be strong or big, that they can figure out a way to make things work. My most recent women's sail-training trip was from Honolulu to Victoria and our crew ranged in age from 18 to 69. That was a great voyage and it's terrific for me too, because it's incumbent upon me as a sailmaker to get out there on the water. It feeds my soul."

Staying on top of technological evolution in the boating world is a challenge, but each year, Hasse has a crash course in the latest developments while serving as one of four judges for the *Cruising World* Boat of the Year competition in Annapolis. "We're given one hour on each of about 30 boats to crawl around them, lift up the sole, check out whatever we can. Then we sail all of them over a four-day period. Very intense. We test all the gear while sailing the boat hard for an hour and then we get off and go to the next boat." After 30 years of being on boats, she says she's developed strong opinions about how things should be organized. For example, although she's seen furling gear for genoas become fairly foolproof, she believes a roller-furling mainsail is "still totally problematic. What I learn over and over again is what we already know: keep it simple, keep it as small as you can and feel comfortable in it." She thinks the most common mistake offshore sailors make is buying a bigger boat than they need and thus ending up with bigger sails. "The size of the boat varies with competency levels, but somewhere in the upper 30s is plenty for most people." She recommends headsails with clews high enough to see under them and to avoid chafe on the pulpit and lifelines. Naturally, she recommends owning a thorough sail inventory: "Something dedicated to light air, and something conservatively sized that's really functional in moderate winds, heavy weather sails including a storm tri-sail, and a working staysail for cutters." She prefers a hanked-on staysail, a storm staysail for winds above 40 knots, a mainsail that can be deeply reefed and, finally, a cruising spinnaker or a drifter. She adapts this advice for other rigs. "I think a big mistake is going with oversized headsails and getting into exotic fibres. They're just not necessary for cruising when you're not trying to get an extra quarter knot, so all of that is money thrown away."

She recounts that when judging new boats in Annapolis last year, she was aboard a high-tech, 65-foot, carbon-fibre-hulled vessel with Kevlar-Mylar sails that could point 20 degrees off the wind and reach at 10.5 knots. Although the million-dollar yacht had the "latest and greatest of everything," she found it an uncomfortable sailer with a difficult deck layout. In contrast, the following day, in the same winds, they tested a 50-foot Herreshoff ketch with a design reaching back to the 1930s, with Dacron sails made by Hasse. That boat didn't point as high into the wind, yet sailed a quarter knot faster than the high-tech model, felt completely comfortable and made for easy sail handling.

Hasse feels fortunate in having trained with a master sailmaker. "We still hand-sew all the grommets along the luff, the foot and the reef points because in the 30 years I've been making sails, I've never seen a hand-sewn ring tear out of a sail. A large hand-worked ring in a mainsail reef cringle will stay in longer because of the flexible surface of the hand stitching. When our sails leave the loft, we expect them to go to New Zealand and back without having the attention of a sailmaker." To make sure the sails the team builds are not only sturdy but have great sail shape, Hasse works with Victoria-based Sandy Goodall, a sailmaker who's specialized in optimizing computer-designed sails. "With all this attention to detail, our sails cost more by a good bit and that's one of the challenges. But I must point out our sails aren't necessarily the ones everyone needs." She explains that when owners of, say, a Hunter 26 call up, she tells them Hasse sails could be overbuilt for their boat.

Boat owners do not have to come to Port Townsend to order Hasse's sails. Besides having a large inventory of sailboat configurations on file, she sends out a thorough measuring form to owners, has a group of trusted "measurers" in various popular sailing grounds and takes dimensions whenever she travels to boat shows and seminars. "One of the neat things about sails," she says, "is that unlike boat builders, if we goof up, we can build a new sail without going bankrupt. Fortunately, in the last 25 years, I don't think we've had to recut eight sails." The dot-com–inspired stock-market shipwreck has influenced the number of orders arriving at Port Townsend Sails. "I'm not interested in turning a huge profit each year," says Hasse, "but I want to keep my 12 employees, pay a living wage, provide health insurance and have a flexible schedule. All my staff are trustworthy, competent artisans."

If Hasse has one regret, it's that she has only one lifetime. "If I had five," she laughs, "I'd homestead in Alaska, run an orphanage in Central America, be an organic gardener in British Columbia and cruise full time. But, of course, I only have one life, so being able to have a home, a big garden and a wooden boat in Port Townsend, do sail training, raise a son, work with kids on the water, teach at schools and seminars, write about sailmaking, empower women with better sailing skills, run a successful business with great staff and be part of a community I love is inspirational. I get to travel and cruise and then come back to a place that's safe and environmentally healthy, where gender equity is as good as it gets. The sea is directing my life's work. I feel blessed."

Martyn Clark
father to a thousand kids

For 18 years, Martyn Clark ran SALTS — the Sail and Life Training Society — a Victoria organization dedicated to giving young people a chance to grow physically, mentally and spiritually while on the water. When 35-year-old Martyn joined SALTS in 1981, he'd already gained significant maritime experience: offshore sailing, shipwrighting, yacht brokering and chartering, and commercial fishing. He'd changed careers and adventures every two or three years. But when he took on SALTS, despite seemingly insurmountable obstacles, including the outfit's near bankruptcy, he stayed for nearly two decades. He persisted for one reason only: the kids.

When signing on with SALTS, Martyn thought he'd hit upon a life of sun and sea, but he quickly learned that to receive a salary, he'd have to raise the funds. He discovered that the sail-training vessel, the *Robertson II*, pumped endless gallons of seawater over the side from the bilges. "The boat wasn't really seaworthy," he recalls. "The SALTS program was faltering and in debt. When I went to get paint, I was met by jaundiced eyes because we hadn't paid our bills." Martyn got out his holystones and went to work. Energetic and accustomed to hard work, he first rebuilt the *Robbie* and made it a safe vessel. From 1981 to 1988, he skippered the sail-training journeys. His wife Marg did much of the cooking for the 30 youthful passengers plus crew. When not aboard with the kids, Martyn fundraised, a task he'd vowed he would never perform. "From my earliest memory, I was a recipient of charity," he says. "I swore that when I grew up, there'd be no begging for me. Yet for 18 years, I did exactly that. God gave me a lesson in humility and I've learned that relying on the generosity of others is not a bad thing."

Martyn was born to missionary parents in 1946 in Peshawar, near the Khyber Pass connecting Afghanistan and (then) India. Nine months later, India gained independence and was partitioned. Most Hindus remained in India, with many Muslims fleeing west and forming Pakistan. In the midst of that deadly turmoil, Martyn's family moved to New Delhi, where they continued their calling. "My mother's parents were also missionaries," says Martyn. "They started off as Anglicans but eventually became affiliated with the Brethren. They're a low-profile group, not much into stained-glass windows, or bowing and scraping. Much like a New Testament church with everybody fairly equal and able to say what they want. Very democratic."

At the age of seven, Martyn followed English custom and headed off to a South India boarding school named Breeks Memorial. "Breeks was created for the offspring of diplomats, missionaries and plantation owners," says Martyn. "It was located in the Nilghiri Hills, called the 'Blue Mountains' because of their eucalyptus trees." Martyn still fondly recalls the little narrow-gauge steam train and its wooden carriages that transported him to school (Breeks still exists). He enjoyed his time there, although when he was 10, he and some other kids ran away, not out of dislike but for the adventure. Martyn, who'd agree with Kipling's statement that "Words are, of course, the most powerful drug used by mankind," thinks he'd been reading too much about Kim, who in Kipling's tale became a child secret service agent. He and his fellow runaways assumed they could sleep in caves, and when they needed food, they'd go to a house at night and raid the fridge. After Martyn got caught, his parents, thinking him unhappy at school, brought him to New Delhi, where he attended a Catholic school with 2,000 boys. "There was lots of structure and I was always getting caned. And for good reason."

Life changed drastically in 1960 when Martyn's parents emigrated to Canada. Martyn was 13 and hated Toronto, where the family chose to live. "I was totally shocked; everyone ice-skated while I'd never seen snow or ice in my life. It was so cold I remember walking to school with three coats on." It took him years to get over the culture shock and to stop feeling like a misfit. But one weekend his dad dragged him off to a youth camp. "I didn't want to go, but he insisted. That's where I met Marg, who was in Grade 11, a year ahead of me." Despite her being an "older woman," they started dating and have never parted. They decided to finish university before marrying and made long-term plans to reward themselves after those many years of courtship with a honeymoon on a schooner.

Martyn's fascination with boats had been stoked by his older brother, Paul, who'd spent summers sailing through B.C.'s Gulf Islands as a deck hand on an old wooden ketch. "Paul had met those renowned sailors the Smeetons and talked non-stop about boats. 'We should sail around the world,' he told me. So I got the bug, read every sailing book I could find and saved my money toward this world trip. Soon, I realized my brother's dream was a pipe dream."

But Martyn's maritime interest had been kindled. By the time he was 18, he'd bought his first boat, *Osprey*, a 25-foot Marconi-rigged sloop. As he was single-minded about being financially autonomous — he was convinced that his parents' missionary and church work made them dependent on charity — he'd obtained after-school jobs as soon as he was able. "I swept up dog dirt at Don Mills Shopping Centre for five years, painted the curbs, cut the lawns." Later, while studying English at the University of Toronto, he worked at Classic Books. At times, however, he played hooky. "If the wind was blowing I'd be down at the bay and jump into *Osprey*." He and first mate Marg made all their sailing mistakes on that little boat: too much sail in a squall and how to dock under sail, because their "horrible, wretched outboard" rarely started.

After graduating from the University of Toronto, it was time for the mythical schooner. Martyn, accompanied by his friend Paul MacKeown, took the train to Halifax. "We only had $7,000 and everyone just laughed at us." Nevertheless, he found a 36-foot, gaff-rigged schooner, *Ayesha,* on Cape Breton. The two lads sailed up the St. Lawrence, and "whatever could possibly go wrong, went wrong." Martyn had bought a rusty sextant for $30 from a man who claimed he had swiped it off the original *Bluenose* before she sank. He also acquired a set of wooden parallel rules and an ancient barometer ("I still have all this old stuff and have used it ever since"), then added a few charts. "It took us forever. We sailed and motored, stuff broke, the engine quit, sand in the diesel. But I remember coming into Toronto Island, seeing this beautiful vision running on the long grass. It was my future wife, Marg, and she'd been waiting for me."

Martyn's father married the couple, and the newlyweds departed on the schooner. They arrived in Cobourg, and Martyn, showing off for his new bride, decided to sail into the dock, a new manoeuvre on *Ayesha.* "So we go screaming in there, round up to the dock and manage to do the thing without too much mishap." A short guy, having watched the shenanigans, ambled over and said, "Either you're a damn fool or you know what you're doing." It was Farley Mowat. In tribute, Mowat offered to make the couple dinner. Mowat was himself cruising on a schooner, *Happy Wanderer,* which later showed up in *The Boat Who Wouldn't Float.* Martyn shyly revealed to Mowat his desire to be a writer. Mowat put him down: "Don't think that just because you want to, you can write." "It took years for me to recover from that blow," says Martyn. That evening, not Farley but an old professor on another vessel cooked the steaks. "Farley didn't do much other than bring a bottle of scotch. I think that's him a little bit, you know."

The honeymooners sailed to Montreal, entered the Richelieu River and Lake Champlain and travelled farther south to New York along the Hudson. The only mishap marring the lovely fall voyage was the gift of old diesel fuel Martyn had gratefully accepted. It wrecked his engine's injectors. "I was poor," he says with a chuckle. The couple eventually made it to the Bahamas and Bermuda. After returning to the Virgin Islands, completely broke, they delivered yachts and offered "some cheap charters." At the end of their honeymoon year, they sold *Ayesha* in Fort Lauderdale.

Back in Toronto, Martyn realized that graduate school would be too tame. "Boats were in my blood." Thus, with his old buddy Paul MacKeown, he founded a yacht brokerage in downtown Toronto on Avenue Road and Bloor Street. "There was only one elderly yacht broker in those days. Now I go there and everyone's a yacht broker." The young men decided on a different tack: the buyer rather than the seller would pay the fee. "So when a buyer came in and wanted a 50-foot schooner, I'd find it for him at the best price. The business took off and I travelled everywhere. Many people wanted a boat and didn't have much money and we knew where cheap boats were. Boats in England — like pilot cutters, Falmouth keypunts and Itchenor ferry cutters — were a quarter of the price they were in Canada." The two entrepreneurs also started a crewed day-sail business with a 1916, 53-foot yawl, *Bernice*. "We were young guys fresh out of school and, with great arrogance, even set ourselves up as marine consultants."

But Marg and Martyn, who had had the first of their five daughters, foresaw the boom in "plastic boats" and figured the traditional vessels they'd specialized in would soon fall out of fashion. Reflecting on their West Indies experience, where bareboat chartering had been introduced, they reckoned that chartering in B.C.'s Gulf Islands might rival the Caribbean. They sold the yacht brokerage to Paul, moved west and built the marina at Maple Bay. They also started Cove Yachts Ltd., first using a charter fleet of Grampians, then shifting to Paceship Yachts, the first trailerable sailboats. By 1973, they had a thriving business, with only Bosun's Charters as competitor.

But success had its drawbacks. "Twenty-three charter boats, the marina, a shipyard doing repairs, a sailing school. One day Marg and I looked at each other and said, 'We never go sailing anymore.' I think there's a great danger for us sailors to do something we love and it gets so big we don't love it anymore. It takes over our lives. So we sold the business."

The idea of sail training for kids had surfaced. Needing a large ship, the intrepid couple, now parents to three daughters, moved to the Isle of Wight and bought a Norwegian Baltic trader, *Nylund*. It was just a hull and they had only six months to completely revamp the boat. The family found the climate and the atmosphere chilly.

Martyn remembers the islanders' outward politeness, but he says, "They were taking bets at the local pub on how many years it'd take."

When the boat was restored — in the prescribed six months — it was too late in the season to cross the Atlantic. They stayed in Dartmouth, where Martyn worked as a shipwright and the boat starred in the films *Water Babies* and *Treasure Island* and in a British television show. The sail-training idea evaporated; they then sold *Nylund* and started scouting for another adventure. Brother Paul proposed commercial fishing as a "way of making a lot of money fast," so the Clarks made their way to Oona River, B.C., a village of 50 souls just south of Prince Rupert.

Martyn did well in the salmon, herring and crab fishing business, but after three years he realized it wasn't his career. He didn't want to be out in the boonies for the rest of his life, and his children were growing up. That was when the call came from SALTS. Martyn only met the organization's board reluctantly because he'd been planning to start his own sail-training business after building a couple of steel-hulled brigantines.

Instead, he inherited the *Robertson II*, a 35-year-old Grand Banks wooden fishing schooner with leaking diesel tanks and an exhaust pipe slung across the deck. To renovate the old dowager, Martyn worked as shipwright part of the day, then shed the overalls, combed his trim captain's beard, donned a tie and, assuming a banker's mien, pleaded for funding from Rotary or Union Club members. Thus, reluctantly, he returned to his once-despised roots and, slowly, the money began to flow. He replaced the *Robbie*'s awkward masts and rig and revamped the ship's interior (the numbered tin mugs and dormitory-style bunks were modelled on his experiences at Breeks). Volunteers showed up to help. SALTS began operating as a business, "not as a woolly-headed charity but as a program that paid for itself."

Over the years, Martyn raised funds for and helped build the *Spirit of Chemainus* (now sold), the *Pacific Swift* (which he captained on its maiden voyage to Australia) and the latest ship, the *Pacific Grace*, which replaced the aged *Robbie*. He "retired" from SALTS in 1999. "I used that word because it made it easy to explain I was leaving. People don't realize the work involved with being the executive director of a large charity. You're endlessly raising money but you get all the complaints. It's not glamorous. I was lucky because I'm a certified master and went out with the kids on the boats as relief skipper. I've talked with a thousand kids. My escape valve."

Retired he's not. In fact, he and Marg have resumed some of their earlier wanderings. "You know, we almost bought a boat in Thailand." They've also set up a consulting business, Clark Maritime, through which they teach workshops and develop curriculums for sail training that still connect them to "the kids." They skipper with SALTS and with an Ottawa sail-training group, and recently spent a year working on *Lynx*, a brand-new sail-training vessel built in Maine. Martyn developed her sail-training program and skippered the vessel to San Diego through the Panama Canal, while Marg was the medical consultant and radio operator.

Martyn is busy developing the curriculum for a Canadian "sailing ship endorsement," which will shortly be required for masters and mates on large sailing ships. "I've collected many old tomes on seamanship as references. All people working on large sailing vessels will have to know such stuff as using a coastal lead line, shifting spars, reefing a topsail, lowering a topsail in a gale and changing jibs in a storm. It'll be a whole new-old chapter in seamanship they can teach the kids and keep them safe."

Reflecting on his adventurous upbringing and life, Martyn remarks that the sea "is never what you expect it to be, but the lessons it imparts really stick with you. The sea has taught me persistence pays off. If you can put up with the privations and hardships of life at sea, the lessons it offers are life changing and that's why it's great for kids. In that way it's mystical.

"For me, the seagoing life has made me a lot more accepting and forgiving. It takes away the greedy side of people. After being at sea on my honeymoon voyage I didn't want to be a business man just earning money for myself. I definitely wanted to do something involving others, sharing the experience. And that's what I've been able to do at SALTS and with sail training — with those kids."

part 2

teak, brass
and glass

The Perfectionist
Like Father, Like Son
Bred in the Bone

Robert Perry
the perfectionist

Robert Perry first sniffed an interest in boats during a junior-high "show and tell." Although he'd never sailed, for some unfathomable reason he chose sailing as his topic, using "a bunch of books" as background. This talk ("I wish I could hear it now," he chuckles) kindled a fever — a fever that has burned unabated since his teenage years — to design cruising yachts that are original, fast and comfortable.

I meet Bob in the unassuming, two-room Seattle office he shares with fellow designer Ben Souquet and two canines, Piper, a 13-year-old Portuguese water dog, and Freda, a 2-year-old German shepherd mix. A pipe rack with 20 well-used pipes hangs among several dozen half-hull models covering the walls. A guitar case leans in a corner. Does he play? "Yeah, a bit of cowboy music." We perch on high stools at the drafting tables, which also support a computer on whose keyboard he types with two fingers, "damn fast, and damn inaccurate too."

"I was a lousy student," begins Bob in his outspoken style. "I was just too busy drawing boats. That's all I did, draw boats." From the age of 14 he knew he wanted to be a yacht designer. He pulls out some of the drawing equipment he's had since that time — three curved plastic tools on which he'd painted white dots to show the utensils were his. During those years, he "memorized" Basil Lubbock's books on clipper ships, which included such romantic titles as *The Opium Clippers* and *The Last of the Windjammers*. He joined the Sea Scouts and learned mechanical drawing. He considered enrolling in the U.S. Coast Guard so he'd be able to sail on its training vessel, the barque *Eagle*, but never signed up for military service. Instead, he studied and drew ships and yachts until their lines became second nature. That's why he is among the world's best-known yacht designers, with more than 5,000 boats of Perry design afloat today.

Bob is tall and lanky, and moves with ease. His black-and-white–checked cotton shirt complements his salt-and-pepper hair and smartly pruned white beard. He was born 57 years ago in Toledo, Ohio, the son of an accountant who'd married an Australian with a yen to go home. Thus Bob's first boat ride was as a toddler on the *Lurline* (freshly reconverted to a passenger liner after serving as a World War II troop carrier) to Sydney, Australia, where he spent the next 11 years. His wasn't a boating family, although his father liked fishing, and Bob has a suitcase full of old snapshots of himself paddling dories and canoes. But, recalls Bob, his dad had a reverence for boats and thought of them as something special. "He taught me how to row, feathering the oars, and how to fish, respecting the fish."

In 1957, a tired old Liberty freighter, the SS *Lakemba*, transported the family from Australia back to North America, where they settled in Seattle. Bob vividly remembers feeling like an immigrant, trying to fit in, striving to leave behind his Aussie accent. "I was an American, you know," he says, "and I didn't want to be a stranger." Shortly afterwards, the 14-year-old delivered his auspicious sailing talk.

"I was lucky," Bob continues. "My geometry teacher, Don Miller, told me to join the Corinthian Yacht Club junior program. He also knew I'd started to draw boats so he told me to take my drawings to Bill Garden, who had his design shop in Seattle." Bob began hitchhiking to Garden's office on Saturday mornings to show his drawings. "Bill neither encouraged nor discouraged me," says Bob. "But he was honest, a genuine guy. I guess the net result was encouragement." The teen also began crewing on Garden's yacht, *Oceanus*, and competed in his first Swiftsure race at 16. "Racing," he says, "teaches you to sail in a heartbeat." He participated in about 20 Swiftsure races until one day he slacked off the sails. "'Hey, I can do this,' I said to myself. 'Do I want to do more? No!'"

Bob feels both gratitude and affection for his mentor. "I really owe an awful lot to Bill." Garden once described all the lawsuits he'd been involved in. "In his quirky way, he was giving me messages," says Bob. "He was real in his advice to me, and if I didn't always want to hear it or buy into it at the time, it was there for me to heed or ignore as I saw fit. He was idiosyncratic but he was kind to me. Kind and honest."

Bob believes that for "eye and originality" there's probably never been a better designer than Bill Garden. Nevertheless, growing up in his shadow had its drawbacks. Bob has always hankered for his own design identity. His quest for an innovative, personal style permeates his conversation. "I had to work consciously not to copy Garden," he explains. "It's like Brahms and Schumann — Brahms is heavily influenced by Schumann, although you don't necessarily hear it in the music. But Brahms can take you through a piece and say, 'Here, here's Schumann.' That's fine and dandy. But I don't want people to look at my stuff and say, 'Here, here's Bill Garden.' I want them to say, 'Here's Bob Perry.' I have digested everything I could from Bill's stuff and tried to re-create it in my own way."

After high school, Bob attended Seattle University, studying mechanical engineering. He didn't flourish in that field and switched to English, but left the university without earning a degree. In 1972, he spent time at Dick Carter's design shop in Nahant, Massachusetts, where he drew IOR boats. But despite the challenging work and such high-powered colleagues as Chuck Paine and Mark Lindsay, Bob re-experienced the loneliness he had felt as a virtual immigrant at the age of 12, so when a commission appeared in Seattle, he moved back and stayed.

A year later, he drew the CT 54, the first of many boats he designed for Taiwanese yards. In fact, when the Taiwanese began expanding their yacht-building industry in the late 1970s and early '80s, he became that island's premier yacht designer, travelling there frequently. He loved the country, the people, the food. He gained "face" by absorbing Chinese business practices and cultural differences, working with the boatyards while they were learning to build quality fibreglass yachts, and mastering enough Mandarin to get along, a talent he shows off when we go to lunch at a Chinese restaurant. (He also discovered in Taiwan that "knockoffs" can be not only clothing and watches, but yachts as well. One of his designs was "stretched" a couple of feet without his receiving credit or royalties.)

In 1974, the Valiant 40 established Bob's reputation as a yacht designer. He also coined the term "performance cruising," which has become synonymous with his work. He invented the expression in part because of the negative reaction he felt to a four-page spread in *Time* magazine, which hailed the Westsail, a Bill Crealock design adaptation, as the ultimate offshore cruising boat. "A lot of the owners knew it was an antiquated design," he says.

"When I designed the Valiant," he continues, "I came up with something the world saw as original. It was a synthesis, a hybrid boat combining racing and cruising elements, which shows an offshore vessel doesn't have to be heavy, with a full keel and a ketch rig." He adds that once you create a label like "performance cruising," it becomes easy for people to recognize the concept. He's proud that the Valiant embodied race-boat ideas of the time and that now, 400 Valiants later, they've been in continuous production longer than any boat in North America. Since the introduction of the Valiant, names like Tayana, Esprit, Nordic, Norseman, Lafitte, Baba, Passport and Saga — all production boats in various lengths — have been added to his résumé.

Can a yacht designer ensure his design is carried out properly? "Let's take the Tayana, of which 600 sold," he replies. "A yard asks me to develop a design. They start building a boat. What if I don't like the way they build it? 'Please do it my way,' I say. 'No, we're doing it our way,' they say. Now I'm stuck. If I tell them they can't build that boat anymore, they can respond, 'We're building it, we've got the moulds.' If I disassociate myself, they say, 'Fine, no more royalties.' It's an ongoing war. You do what you can to make the yard conform to your specs, but in the end, the yard always wins."

Bob has concentrated on sailboat design because powerboats don't appeal to him emotionally. He also eschews mega-yachts because they require a design team, and that, in his view, fragments the design integrity. Although he's recently designed the production sailboats Saga 42 and 35, most of his contemporary work consists of one-off designs, including a $7-million submarine two years ago. A sub? "The client wanted it. I judge the success of the design by the client's satisfaction."

Over the years, Bob has received several honours, including the Medal of Achievement for Performance Cruising Design from *Yacht Racing/Cruising Magazine* and induction into *Cruising World*'s Cruising Hall of Fame. He laughs about being a Hall of Famer. *"Cruising World* put me in with a whole bunch of dead people. I ignored the award party, but I'm proud of the honour. You know what they say: You are what they say you are."

What really counts for Bob is peer recognition from other designers in his class, although he doesn't reveal who he considers are at his level. Peer recognition, he says, balances out the "detractors and the asskissers." He jokes that one website published such fawning commentary on his boats that he was forced to attack himself using the pseudonyms "Clifton Clowers" and "Capt. Crotchmaple." It worked. Shortly afterwards, the website began to assail Bob's designs in earnest.

Despite his 30 years in the design business, Bob still strives to perfect his work and believes he's slowly getting better and better. That's one reason he rarely sells old yacht plans. "I don't want to sell things I did 15 years ago. I wouldn't do a single thing the same way. I want to make new designs, superior designs." Moreover, he's concerned about home-built boats that bear no resemblance to his original drawings. "These boats are built in a garage and can be hideous. And the builders plaster my name all over it!" To prevent these catastrophes, he puts a high price on any yacht plans he does sell which, he estimates, gets rid of the "wankers."

One day Bob saw a badly written review of one of his boats. With characteristic aplomb and directness, he called *Sailing* and said, "Jesus, even I could write better than that." The editor invited him to try. Thus, for 25 years, Bob has written reviews of four boats each month: The reviews have been collected and published in five books. His prose is frank and mimics his speech: plain-spoken, with a grin but an edge of curtness. He likes having his voice and opinions out there. "It's a bit of an ego thing," he declares, "but I think I'm doing it better than anyone. There may be better people, but they're not writing the reviews."

Bob offers clear advice to young people wanting to become yacht designers. "Get a degree, preferably in engineering." He mentions mechanical or materials engineering, or architectural design, as specialty areas. Besides, he chuckles, these fields give aspiring designers something to fall back on — a real job. "After the degree, enroll at a place like Westlawn [Westlawn School of Yacht Design in Stamford, Connecticut], where students are forced to study all the things that aren't easy to learn on their own." As an example, he cites a weight study Ben Souquet is conducting on a 70-foot boat. "That's the most arduous, most demanding job of any design. More than math. It requires the designer to assign weights to every component of a new boat so the vessel will sit on its designed waterline."

One topic Bob doesn't contemplate is retirement. "It would be torture." He has no wish to retire, ever. Rather, he's still like the teenager drawing boats — he just wants to draw more of them. "I'm always dissatisfied and aware that my designs could be better. I don't know how good boats can be. There must be limits, but I don't know where they are."

For relaxation, Bob sails *Perrywinkle*, his Swedish-built Cirrus 7.8, and studies the lives of the great composers. An audiophile preferring the fidelity of records to digitized CDs, he sprinkles his speech with references to classical music. I ask who he'd be if he were a composer and we debate the merits of Mozart, Mendelssohn and Mahler. I propose the grand operatic life of Verdi, but his response is emphatic: "Scarlatti. Domenico Scarlatti. He's mysterious and abstruse."

When I telephoned Bob Perry for an interview, he agreed to meet me but spoke with a hint of brusquerie. "Don't ask me any personal questions," he said grouchily. "I only talk about boat design." But his seeming crustiness hides a softer side and a sense of humour. A Seattle yacht broker tells me he received a call from a gruff caller demanding to know what boats were on the block. When the broker mentioned a Perry design, the caller said, "I don't want to hear about his boats. They're terrible and the designer is an asshole." The broker paused. "Bob?" he queried.

Bob teaches drawing to his wife Jill's Grade 3 classes, and some of the kids paint sailboats on the briny. He's a concerned father to sons Spike and Maxwell. And he recently spoke at the memorial service of a fan who'd been too timid to ever speak to him directly. "I want people to know I'm approachable," he says. "People can talk to me. At a boat show, that's why I'm there. I love people to speak to me when I'm standing around."

Bent and Eric Jespersen
like father, like son

For the first nine years after opening his wooden-boat building yard on the waterfront in Sidney, B.C., Bent Jespersen had no telephone. If he needed to connect with customers or suppliers, he'd walk home for lunch and call them from there. No one seemed to mind his "high noon" methods. "Everyone got used to my calling during the lunch hour," recalls Bent. "For me, it was great. No telephone to interrupt the work. And very cost effective." He finally installed a single line only because the pregnant wife of one of his employees wanted access to her husband.

Throughout his life, Bent has exhibited similar practicality, looking for ways to limit overhead, getting his chosen work done without intrusions, asking others to see it his way. Perhaps these characteristics have contributed to an international reputation for incorporating modern materials and methods into traditional wooden-boat building. Since 1974, most of the boats constructed at Jespersen Boatbuilders have used the cold-moulding process, in which laminated, crisscrossed layers of wood create a hull that is watertight, strong, stiff and lightweight. Modern epoxy resins (unheated, hence the name "cold moulded") bond the wooden layers and have substituted for the hot glues used in the 1940s and '50s. "The disadvantage of a traditionally built wooden boat," explains Bent, "is that it soaks up water from the moment it's launched, swells up and forces the fasteners. When it dries out again, everything is loose and that's why these boats deteriorate."

Bent's renown has grown despite the fact that he, and now his son Eric, Olympic medallist and world champion sailor, who took over the company reins eight years ago, have chosen to remain a modestly sized business. When asked how they survived various recessions over the past quarter century — hard economic times have habitually snuffed out boat builders even more than other entrepreneurs — they say they were not affected. Bent explains many boat builders expand during a boom, and when the inevitable downturn comes, they can't meet the overhead costs. For Jespersen, the commissions have just kept coming, one at a time. Their list of one-off designs is impressive. Jespersen has built Laser designer Bruce Kirby's six- and eight-metre sailracers, classic Baltic traders, a Peterson-designed, 41-foot offshore racer, cruising sailboats, a series of Bill Garden designs, schooners, pilot boats, and a cornucopia of other powerboats, sailboats and dinghies. During Eric's tenure, the company has expanded its boat repair and refit business. "The staff prefer to build new boats," says Eric. "But new boats are expensive and not that many are being commissioned. And I like to keep the wooden boats already out there afloat. They're much rarer now in a sea of fibreglass vessels."

The father-and-son marine tradition started well before the present shop in Sidney. Bent grew up in northern Denmark, in the town of Aalborg on the Limfjorden. He left school at 15 and apprenticed at the local shipyard — the largest employer in town — where his dad, older brother and uncle were already employed. He completed his ship's carpenter training four years later. "I enjoyed it. I worked from 7:00 A.M. until 4:30 P.M., six days a week. Three evenings I attended technical classes. There sure wasn't any time for mischief," he says in his Danish-accented voice. After finishing their apprenticeships, most of Bent's young colleagues went into military service. Bent reflected that if he stayed in Denmark and served in the navy, he'd probably find someone to marry and never satisfy his yearning for travel. "I decided to leave. I was keen on Australia, but it was far and costly. I had just enough money to go to Toronto." The 19-year-old arrived there in 1955, and after saving a few dollars, moved to New Westminster, B.C., where he joined a shipyard that built tugs and barges. One day, he discovered that pulp mill construction in Port Alberni paid carpenters more. "They hired a couple of thousand workers, mostly Europeans and immigrants. And there I met Jannie, who worked at the hospital. She was from Holland and we married."

Eventually, he received a job offer from Philbrook's in Sidney, where he worked as a boat builder from 1962 to 1971. By now a father of four, he hadn't lost his taste for travel. Bent was offered a United Nations position to teach boat design and boat building in Ghana on its huge, man-made Lake Volta. "I didn't know where Ghana was since it was called the Gold Coast when I grew up. But I looked at a map, discussed it with Jannie and after 10 minutes we decided to go. We figured if it was under the United Nations, it couldn't be that bad." Bent found it an interesting job to teach Ghanaian fishermen to build a better canoe. "It was a simple 24- to 26-foot vessel based on the dory, three planks high with a cross-plank bottom, something easily constructed without machinery." He's been told by recent visitors to Ghana that many of today's fishing boats resemble the ones they built in the early 1970s.

Eric remembers the 18 months there as a valuable life experience. "I was 11, and it changed my perspective dramatically," he says. "For the first time, I was the minority. It was good to leave my peer group here and come back and reassess everything. The stay set a high standard for our family, doing things that other families wouldn't do. We learned not to be afraid of new things and to have lofty goals."

After returning to Vancouver Island, Bent took back his job as foreman at Philbrook's, but things had changed. The yard had switched to making fibreglass patrol boats, not the kind of boat building Bent relished. Then he was approached by a local physician, Les Horne, who wanted a one-off wooden boat. Philbrook's declined the job, so Bent quit and opened shop — not to become an entrepreneur, mind you; just to build that one boat. But afterwards, as Bent puts it, "there was just one boat after another." He credits yacht designer Bill Garden, who lives in the neighbourhood, with being helpful in building the business. "Bill could pull a client out of his pocket at any time. He's always been good in that if someone started up a shop, he'd put some work their way. If he liked the work, he'd send more. He preferred his projects to be close so he could keep his eye on them without travelling. If there was a question, I'd phone and he'd stop by in the morning and we'd sort it out."

Along the way, Bent's family was growing up. They sailed together, all six of them, on a Herreshoff 28, cruising up to Desolation Sound and around Vancouver Island. Later, his two daughters, Karen and Julie, rowed competitively, while son Peter preferred canoes. Eric was always interested in boats, boat building and racing. He started sailing when he was six and was competing at eight. He hung around the marina and did jobs for everyone but his dad, who couldn't have his son "holding onto his coattails." Eric towed and hauled boats, and when he reached the age of 16, he was hired by Philbrook's. He also worked in the summer on salmon trollers. When Eric returned from commercial fishing, Bent, fearing his son would blow his earnings on some beat-up car, made a prophetic proposition: They'd build a Star as a father-and-son team. Bent would supply the materials, Eric the rig.

Eric raced the Star, but his first chance at high-level racing came when Canada entered the America's Cup challenge in 1982. Eric was 21 years old, and big. At 6 foot 2 inches and 240 pounds, he towers over his slender, more compact parents. "I've heard the Dutch had to be tall to look over the top of the dike and keep their heads above water," he jokes. "George Wilkins was recruiting experienced sailors from coast to coast, and eventually I was hired as one of the crew members on *Canada I*, designed by Bruce Kirby. I went to the training camp in Florida to learn about 12-metre boats. My boat-building background came in handy and I helped finish and rig the boat."

Eric also discovered something that "saved Kirby's bacon." While working on the keel's trim tab, he noticed that the fitting hung down a quarter-inch below the rest of the keel. He knew instantly that the tiny protrusion would violate the boat's 12-metre rule, and that the extra draft would be paid for by reduced sail area. "Kirby was alarmed," Eric recalls, grinning. "The measurer was coming at 0700, so I worked all night, shortened the trim tab and recessed the fitting. Fortunately, the boat measured to the millimetre for maximum draft. What I learned from this event is that boat builders must make designers look good. After that, Kirby was always firmly supportive of me and my sailing endeavours."

Eric, then 22, sailed in the America's Cup on *Canada I* , which came in fourth among the challengers, an experience he calls "getting a master's degree in sailing. All the experts and the best sailors in Canada came down to sail with us. It was a chance to learn from all those guys and I really improved my skills and general knowledge of the whole sailing world." Four years later, he and Bent were involved in modifying *Canada I* into *Canada II* by adding a wing keel and new rudders. In the 1987 America's Cup in Australia, *Canada II* came in seventh.

Eric returned home, married and, while sailing in a little regatta in 1991, was asked to participate in the Star Olympic trials held in Vancouver. Eric agreed. A year later, in the 1992 Barcelona Olympics, he and sailing partner Ross MacDonald won a bronze medal. (Eric recalls a bit wryly that "all my friends and family said afterwards, 'Oh, we didn't think you could do that.'") The teammates decided to keep sailing, with the goal of earning gold four years later. In anticipation, they won three championships: the World, European and North American contests, followed by the Western Hemisphere win. Eric was named "Male Athlete of the Year" by the Canadian Yachting Association. "We were really on a roll starring on our Star. But when we got to the Atlanta Olympics in 1996, we learned there were disadvantages to being number one in the world. We were the ones to beat. We had protest problems — it was in everyone's interest to see us with a disqualification, which we received the first day. Then we had an 'over early start' and ultimately a poor finish." Nevertheless, all this training, which Eric calls his sailing PhD, was a wonderful experience. After that, he designed and built his own 30-foot vessel, which he has sailed with his wife, Anne, his 10-year-old daughter, Emma, and eight-year-old son, Ross.

In 1994, between Olympic competitions and the other championships, Bent retired and Eric took over the firm. "When a boat builder says he wants to retire, he better do it quickly, before he loses everything," Bent quips. "Really, I had enough savings and Eric was ready. I wanted to travel with Jannie." The couple has visited Holland and Denmark and made a recent trip to the island on the other side of the continent, Newfoundland.

Is it difficult to be an SOB, a son of a boss? It has its trials, admits Eric. As a kid, he recalls being intimidated by his father's skills with wood and being afraid to touch tools. "I coped by learning different things," says Eric. "I know more about mechanical and electrical systems, which interest Dad less." When he took over the business, it was awkward for some of the long-term staff to see Eric as the new boss. Between father and son, the transition has been fairly smooth, in part because it was rapid, and because Bent only sticks in his oar when asked. "I'm lucky to have a father I can work with," says Eric. "He's the easygoing one. I hear people talk about working with their father and how easy it is to rub each other the wrong way. For us, our common interests have been more important than anything. We've enjoyed it together."

Eric mimics his dad in his business approach, focussing on quality and good customer relationships. He continues traditional wooden-boat building using modern materials, and works in the same simple shop, with its big windows, power and hand tools, and thick golden globs of dried resin splotching the floor. "We're purists," he wisecracks, "we use pure epoxy." He adds that he plans to keep the firm's size sensible. He built a 63-foot powerboat, which required two shops and a much larger crew. "That was successful," he says, "and I did it so I could say I did it. But it wasn't all that enjoyable. Basically, the infrastructure for managing a larger crew wasn't there. You can manage seven guys by yourself if they're self-directed, but with a larger crew, you need a foreman type and office staff. I never really took those steps, so that made it hard. And on top of that, customers get harder nosed as prices go up."

Although Bent doesn't go into the shop unless invited, the father-and-son duo recently completed a two-year refit on *San Mateo*, a 41-foot fish boat. Naturally, it's a wooden boat, built in 1957. The vessel was structurally sound, but the Jespersens wanted to make her into a comfortable, family cruising vessel, taking her far beyond her original fishy purpose. It was a big job. After removing all the fishing gear, they scraped out dirt and fish blood, and cut out the fibreglass and foam-lined hold that stored the fish. The fish hold now houses the main saloon, topped by a cheerful deck house with portholes all around. The goal was to maintain the lines of the west-coast troller, not convert her into a yacht. "If you start building huge houses on these fish boats, they just don't look right," Bent declares. It worked. The boat looks spiffy, offers comfort — although in typical Jespersen fashion, nothing is ostentatious — has lost any vestige of fishy smells, and was exhibited at Victoria's Classic Boat Festival. Eric also valued the collaborative aspect of revamping the 45-year-old boat. "We had a deal where he supplied the labour and I provided the materials. Every day over coffee, we collaborated over the design, and bit by bit, we worked our way through the different areas. This teamwork was outside of the business, and it's important that it happened that way."

Eric says the sea has been his whole life. "Total domination, basically." He cites his seafaring background on his father's side and reveals, "If I can't smell the sea I get nervous. Even on my days off I come to the marina because I love boats, something I've always done naturally. Other than family, it's the most important thing. The only thing." Yet he sees his relationship with the sea as still at the beginning. He expects to continue Jespersen Boatbuilders, but would like to do some ocean racing and single-handed racing. "I'm not sure how I'm going to do it, but I never worried in the past. I just dreamed big and let the details work themselves out."

Bent may claim he's retired, but he continues doing what he likes best: working with wood near the ocean. He has a workshop in his garage and has built and carved models for Victoria artist Roland Brener, artifacts that are now in a museum. "I often joke

that if I hadn't had so much fun I could have made a lot of money,"
he concludes. "But I've had a good life and I wouldn't want to
have done anything else. And I'm still doing what I love. You
know, I keep thinking of a story about the Canadian comedy
team Wayne and Schuster. Their agent kept urging them to go
to Vegas and earn a fortune. They said they were happier staying
at home. 'Happiness isn't everything,' exclaimed their agent. But
he was wrong. As I said, I might have made much more money if
I'd had less fun. But fun is more important. They don't tax you
on the fun and that's our way to outwit the tax collector."

Ted Brewer
bred in the bone

"**D**esigning boats is an ego trip. It's gratifying to design just one more, even if 90 percent of the plans never get built. Those drawings are for dreamers."

Edward S. Brewer should know. He's been dreaming about boats since his childhood in Hamilton, Ontario. And that's why he continues designing in his cedar-clad retirement home on B.C.'s Gabriola Island, where he lives with his wife, Betty, a registered nurse. Despite plans to rest on his oars, the bulky 69-year-old still spends most days creating plans for yet another model and printing out the line drawings on his plotter. His designs now number more than 270. All of them can be purchased as study or complete plans.

Boaters around the globe know the names: Aloha 28/34, Atlantic 45, Grand Banks 22, Quickstep 24, Cabot 36, Jason 35, Goderich 35, Hullmaster 27/31, Lazyjack 32, Murray 33, Whitby 42/55, Morgan 38, Tree of Life 68, Islander 48, Sea Star 46, Deer Isle 28 and many more. For his personal cruising, fishing and crabbing, Ted designed the Nimble Nomad motor cruiser. Cat boats, sloops, dories, sharpies, schooners, racers, trawlers, yawls, ketches, cutters, skiffs. Steel, fibreglass, aluminum, wood. Is there anything in boat design Ted hasn't put his mind to? "Yes," he says, "ferro-cement."

For Ted, boating is bred in the bone. His father, Edward J. Brewer ("Old Ted"), began his career in the Canadian Merchant Marine and sailed around the world before he married. "Young

Ted" Brewer was born in Hamilton in 1933 and started boating early. "I remember going to the lodge on Katchanwanooka Lake and operating the runabout when I was 11," Ted recalls smilingly. "My dad had become chief on the navy's HMCS *Star*, and by age 16, I was taking out the navy's 26-foot sailing yawls. I also raced dinghies."

In Ted's high school yearbook, his classmates, knowing about Ted's proclivities, predicted he'd be "most likely to end up in a watery grave." When he was 15, he and a schoolmate were determined to learn scuba diving. Roaming around a junkyard, they searched for a copper instrument they could convert into a diving helmet. Ted still snickers at the memory. "When the owner heard what we were hunting, he whipped out this old copper deep-sea helmet and weighed it. 'Thirty pounds,' he said. 'That'll be nine bucks.'" The teenagers attached 100 feet of garden hose to the helmet. Using a couple of tire pumps, one would dive down about 30 feet, while the other pumped. "My high school friends thought I was a nut. The diving, and then capsizing a sailboat in Hamilton Bay ... "

After high school, Ted served in the Canadian army for five years, rising to the rank of lieutenant; he spent his time serving on Lake Simcoe, skippering 16-foot cruisers down the Trent-Severn Canal and scuba diving with proper equipment. Although Ted enjoyed army life, a superior officer, knowing Ted had signed up for a correspondence course at the Westlawn School of Yacht Design, told him to concentrate on what he loved best. In 1957, Ted resigned his commission and began a three-year stint as yacht broker under George Cuthbertson with Canadian Northern Co., now C&C Yachts. He raced eight-metre yachts on Lake Ontario and sailed his own small craft throughout the region. He also continued with his Westlawn correspondence program and studied in his spare time. "Westlawn had trained designers for 70 years and their three-year program was no picnic. I only took Saturday night off from studying." He graduated in 1960.

His break came the same year when he joined Bill Luders Marine Construction in Connecticut, a medium-sized yard that had built ships as big as minesweepers during the Korean War, but was then concentrating on Gold Cup sailboat designs and on the hot 5.5-metre Olympic class, popular with such famous sailors as George O'Day and Ted Turner. Ted worked on boats of all sizes and helped convert the 12-metre *Weatherly*, a defender in the 1962 America's Cup, into a cruising boat. He drew the 12-metre *American Eagle* and supervised her construction. Weekends he raced on Luders' *Storm*. He also crewed on Luders' designs in long-distance races. "Those were great years," Ted reflects wistfully. "These yachtsmen raised money privately through syndicates. That was before every yacht was slathered with advertising. I don't even read about them today."

Ted recalls his years at Luders' yard with great fondness. "I was doing a lot of my own work under Bill, but he was a mentor to me. I owe him everything. I thought I knew things until I worked for him. He was tops." Ted also liked being in a yard where the boats were constructed. "There's nothing like being able to talk with the people doing the actual work."

When Luders reduced his workload, Ted relocated to Brooklin, Maine (now home to the WoodenBoat School), and launched his own design shop. "Bill Luders referred lots of work to me in the beginning," he says. "It really helped to get me started in the business." He spent the next dozen years in Maine, building his firm and becoming known for sturdy, moderate- to heavy-displacement cruising designs, which focussed on performance, manoeuvrability and speed. His designs ranged from 18-foot catboats to a 64-foot, three-masted schooner intended for day sailing. He pioneered his "radius bilge" method of building metal hulls, applying it in dozens of steel and aluminum vessels. This technique is used by most designers today. To stay in trim, he entered three Transpacific Yacht Races and has cruised the eastern Mediterranean, the Caribbean and the Pacific Northwest.

In 1976, Evergreen State College in Olympia, Washington, invited him as guest speaker at a "fishing under sail" seminar. "I fell in love with this coast," enthuses Ted. "I was a rock climber and wanted to conquer the Olympics. I also met yacht designer Bob Perry, who became a long-term friend." A year later, Ted rode from Maine to Washington on his Suzuki Water Buffalo motorbike to reconnoitre the Pacific Northwest one more time. "I sold my Maine operation and settled in Anacortes, Washington." There, he continued designing custom and production cruisers for two more decades.

He also wrote his first of three books. Two are now out of print, but *Understanding Boat Design*, which started as course notes for his own yacht-design program, is in its fourth edition. In it, he explains the elements that go into designing boats: "Regardless of type, every boat is a compromise between four basic factors: seaworthiness, comfort, performance and cost. You cannot hope to obtain more of any one of these factors without sacrificing some of the others."

Among all his 270-plus designs, he's proudest of *Tree of Life*, a 70-foot, Nova Scotia-built schooner that won the 2000 Antigua Race Week. Another favourite is the 43-foot *Black Velvet*, a strip-planked custom design launched in 1970. Its success evolved into the highly popular Whitby 42, of which about 400 were built.

Reflecting on boat design over his lifetime, Ted sees the revolution in materials as the most significant transformation. "When I started in the 1960s, it was wood. Now, besides fibreglass, we have carbon fibre, epoxies, different metals. And that's only for the hull and rigging." He notes that wood had been the only boat material for thousands of years, while new technologies are showing up so fast they're hard to track and analyze.

Similarly, the profession of yacht design has changed significantly in the last decades. "It's much more complicated today. There are the mega-yachts, for example. If you want to design those, you should attend the naval architecture programs at MIT or the University of Michigan. But if you want a nice little business, you can still study with Westlawn. Computers have eliminated some of the grunt work; you can feed in the numbers. Although, be warned — computers don't save you as much time as you think. But they do allow you to experiment more." He adds that hands-on training continues to be crucial. He advises aspiring designers to get their hands dirty, work with good builders and work with a variety of craftsmen.

Ted and Betty decided to leave Anacortes because it had become too "boutiquey." He professes to hate cities, shopping, crowds and flying. "We'd been looking around the Gulf Islands for some time," Ted says, his gravelly voice betraying his fondness for what he calls "40 years of making fine cigarette ashes" (Betty made him quit 12 years ago). "Then in 1998, we were cruising to Silva Bay and saw one of my Whitbys. I picked up a local paper and learned real estate was much less expensive and Social Security goes a lot further on this island. Betty already had her B.C. nursing licence so we moved here. For us, it's paradise."

But paradise is a busy place. Besides designing the occasional new boat and selling older drawings from his half-hull–decorated office, he volunteers at Gabriola's Silva Bay Shipyard, teaching boat building techniques. "I don't teach these guys how to design, but to distinguish. I want them to know why this hull shape is good, that one poor. About fairing properly. They should be able to design small parts. There's a future for both designers and builders."

He also travels to various boat festivals where he judges vessels, attends some of the rendezvous of his boats, writes articles for several boating magazines and has started composing his memoirs. He enlarges his collection of marine tomes and World War I books and, through Betty, has added five grandchildren to his life. They are responsible for a revival of a childhood passion for model trains. "I had a Lionel set when I was 10," he says. "In Maine, I had a huge layout. But I sold it all." Then he saw a train ad and said to himself, "It'll be cute to have a train around the Christmas tree for the grandkids." He's now invested in 70 freight cars and eight engines and has graded portions of his backyard to support long sections of track. The grandchildren call him "Grandpa Train."

One day, looking at the rails, he recognized the need for a model railroad building. Drawing on decades of experience, he quickly sketched a building with pen and ink on Mylar, blueprinted it and added model railroad buildings, grain silos and train stations to his sales of boat plans. Ibec Wood of Cobble Hill now produces cedar-log kits based on Ted's designs.

Ted is satisfied. "We're happy as clams here on our island," he concludes. "And designing boats has given me a great life. I've never been rich, but I've enjoyed my profession. I've sailed, raced, travelled. Seen the world. Met wonderful people. How else could I have gone to see a 60-foot yacht being built on a mountaintop in Guatemala?"

part 3

adventurers
and eccentrics

The River Runner
The Hermit
In the Teeth of the Wind
Salt of all Trades
Into Thick Air

Colin Angus
the river runner

By the time he was 30, Colin Angus had sailed as far as New Zealand and Papua New Guinea on his own sailboat, survived a cross-continental rafting expedition down the treacherous Amazon, and pulled off a 3,750-mile kayaking-rowing voyage down the Yenisey River from its Mongolian source to its mouth in the Siberian Arctic.

Colin's sense of adventure had been kindled early by books. In Grade 5, he encountered Robin Lee Graham's autobiography, *Dove*. "Here he was, circumnavigating the world when he was only 16," says Colin, still aroused by the memory. "All those tropical islands, the lifestyle. I lived in Port Alberni, a mill town on Vancouver Island, and Robin's globetrotting seemed so exotic. I then read all the dusty seafaring book on the back shelves at the public library. They taught me the lore and terminology. I decided that one day I'd set my own sails."

When you look at Colin, with his sea-blue eyes and slender build, you marvel that he and his two mates frequently portaged their 600-pound raft and gear over rough terrain flanking the upper Amazon's most lethal white-water rapids. But under his tanned skin, the muscles are long and sinewy. And as he recounts his tales of derring-do, it's clear his mind is just as muscular.

Colin grew up the fourth child in a single-parent family with strapped finances. His Edinburgh-born mother taught school and, according to Colin, was a true example of Scottish thrift. Although he sometimes views his mom's economies with a smidgen of youthful disparagement, Colin learned valuable money skills — skills he has applied throughout his exploits. By the time he was 12, he had launched his first savings account with a paper route, so when the family moved to Comox four years later, Colin emptied his piggybank and bought a day-sailing dinghy "to learn the physics of sailing." To finance his studies at the University of British Columbia, he worked summers on a fish boat. One afternoon, from his third-floor English class, he gazed at the freighters, fish boats and sailboats moving around sun-streaked Vancouver Harbour and had a spiritual flash: time's a-wasting. He quit school.

Colin has strong opinions about travelling — for him, it's more than hopping on a plane and emerging in a new country. "That's hardly more arduous than driving up Vancouver Island or the I-5. For me, travelling and exploring include awareness: you must put the work, energy, preparation and survival into the actual travelling process. That's one reason for going off in a sailboat."

To speed up his sailing departure, he pooled resources with a high-school buddy, Dan Audet. Colin planted trees; Dan washed dishes and worked in a museum. In 1992, the two 20-year-olds found a 27-foot Huntingford, *Ondine*, "a heavy, narrow boat. She got us there, but she definitely wasn't a performance cruiser; you could barely get 90° to the wind. But she only cost $15,000. Not much luxury, but we did get GPS and a sextant as backup." By the time they reached San Francisco, they were broke, so they worked on other people's boats and held odd jobs. "We liked living the 'sailing lifestyle' and earned enough to hop down the coast to Mexico." After adding a self-steering windvane (they'd learned how exhausting steering can be), they eventually arrived in the Marquesas Islands of French Polynesia with only $75 in their pockets. "It was a real-life *Survivor*. But there's lots of fish and fruit in the Marquesas and we bought some rice." After passaging to Tahiti, they were hired by the captain of the 207-foot *Virginian*, a $100-million dollar yacht with a helicopter landing pad, owned by John Kluge of Orion Pictures. "I was a deck hand, part of a 13-man crew maintaining the vessel. Kluge wasn't there often. We'd been living like savages off the land, then, suddenly, exchanged our cockroachy wooden vessel for a cabin with a stereo, TV, and ensuite hot shower. Even a chef to cook for us. Sheer decadence."

Colin worked on the luxury yacht for nine months, bought *Ondine* outright and single-handed to New Caledonia and then Australia. After hitchhiking through the Outback and experiencing "a homeless incident, sleeping in ditches and eating out of dumpsters" when his ATM card malfunctioned, he sailed to New Zealand. "By now, like Robin Lee Graham, I'd travelled for about five years and that's what I'd wanted to do." So he sold the boat and sailed to Port Moresby, Papua New Guinea, where the new owner took possession. Colin travelled in Europe, worked in London and then returned to Canada to prepare for the next task he'd set himself: a self-propelled journey across South America. He planned to start on foot at the Pacific, trek over the continental divide to the Amazon's source and then raft to its Atlantic mouth. "South America always fascinated me. I was intrigued by the jungle and the world's largest river. But I wanted more than just to go there — I wanted a bit of a theme, a challenge. I'd been reading a bunch of books, and Joe Kane's *Running the Amazon*, which documented the first successful descent in 1986, grabbed me totally." (Several other attempts ended with deaths and serious injuries — only two succeeded before Colin's.)

Colin recruited two daredevils he'd met in London to join him on his Amazonian quest: Australian Ben Kozel, 26, and Scott Borthwick, 23, of South Africa. They pooled their funds, though no one could say the trip was overfinanced. The entire five-month voyage, including the 13-foot inflatable raft, supplies, tents, transportation to Peru, internal travel and hotels, food, camera and film, cost only $17,000. "Most people just cannot believe that," says Colin, "but you see people from third-world countries living on budgets of much less."

As it was impossible to carry their rafting gear and supplies across the Andes, they'd flown the equipment to the old Inca capital, Cuzco, located nearer the Amazon's source. Their on-foot journey began on September 11, 1999, with the trio dipping their toes into the ocean at Camana, a Peruvian village north of the Chilean border. While hiking to the river's source, they lugged 66-pound packs. The trek nearly took their lives. Underestimating the length of the desert climb and relying on outdated maps (the only ones available), they ran out of water. Altitude sickness, combined with freezing temperatures and near starvation, weakened them. Despite the hardships, they eventually reached the source of the Amazon's longest tributary, the Apurimac, at 18,000 feet and faced 4,142 miles of river before they would reach the Atlantic.

In his book, *Amazon Extreme*, Colin concludes his narrative of the turbulent,150-day voyage with these words: " ... our trip was ending on a magical note. It felt good. Damn good." But after I had read the tale that led to these words and had listened to his telling me about it, the expedition seems to be a string of terror, dangerous rapids, illness, insect attacks, hunger, fatigue, fear and anxiety.

The Apurimac is one of the world's most treacherous rivers, which descends 12,800 feet over only 375 miles. A rating scale classifies many rapids on this section as "sixes." Sixes are extreme — white water filled with cataracts, chutes, killer holes, boils, boulder sieves and standing waves. To avoid death, the rafters tried to assess the rapids ahead of them, plan the best approach or portage around the worst stretches. Progress was slow, often only three miles a day. "You're spending all your time with this massive roar of spray and foam. If you portage, the terrain is rough, with cliffs, boulders and scree. The scariest was when the cliffs fell straight into the river and the water in between was just a maelstrom. You'd be forced to run the rapids. And the whole floor of the canyon is massive boulders, with the river flowing through them. But it's a trap, a sieve — the water can pour through, but a body gets jammed. That's where you die."

When the trio finally travelled beyond the rapids (it took six weeks), they transformed the raft into a rowboat by tying paddles to bamboo stakes and adding balsa wood beams on which they slept, although life didn't get much easier. While they rowed in shifts so they could move 24 hours a day, blackflies, mosquitoes and other biting insects harassed them; parasitic illnesses plagued them; rain forest downpours and sweat rotted the clothing on their backs; sores and lesions pockmarked their skin in the endless damp. Shining Path guerrillas shot at them, and Peruvian military mistook them for guerrillas and also spat bullets their way. Some villagers were hospitable, others threatening.

Yet despite — or maybe because of — these hardships and trials, Colin is deeply satisfied to have completed the journey on his own power. "My companions were excellent and you always learn about yourself. On the river we met the happiest and most genuine kind of people. And I have a definite sense of accomplishment." After returning home, he wrote his book and cut a documentary video. And he began planning the next event: descending the world's fifth-longest river, the Yenisey. Thirteen months after completing his Amazon gamble, he was back in a boat.

This time he found some sponsors who provided a raft, two river kayaks, satellite phones and Gore-Tex clothing for the five-month venture down the 3,725-mile river. The trip began in April, just after the river melted, and had to be completed before the fall freeze. He travelled initially with two others, his Amazon cohort, Ben Kozel, and Remy Quinter. The voyage's expense grew to $60,000.

The team flew to Mongolia's capital, Ulaanbaatar, and then rented a jeep to take them the first part of the 600 miles toward the river's source. They drove through the countryside (no roads), camped at night, then hiked to the Yenisey's source at 13,000 feet on the Otgon Tenger in the Hangayn Mountains and followed the icy trickle until it broadened sufficiently for the team to launch the rowing raft and kayaks.

After getting through the worst of the white water — nothing as bad as the Amazon — the trio was heading into a meandering valley when another tributary, in flood, joined their stream. "It didn't seem dangerous and we were just hooting along until we ran into a sweeper tree. That's a tree still on the bank but leaning out with all its lower branches in the water." The raft caught and capsized, and in the ripping current, some gear floated away.

They captured the bag containing passports, but the most vital dry bag, safeguarding the film for the documentary they'd sold to *National Geographic*, freewheeled down the river. Colin liberated a neon-yellow kayak, jumped in wearing only a pair of pants and paddled furiously after the precious bag, hoping to catch it. He assumed his mates would appear within hours.

No one showed up for 12 days.

Colin had a lighter and a multi-tool in his pants' pocket, but no food, shelter or clothing. Night temperatures dipped to freezing. To survive, he cooked stinging nettles and rhubarb. He shivered and worried. When he saw Mongolian herders on shore, he hesitated before hailing them. "What would they think of this guy who didn't speak their language, coming up from the river half-naked? So I just tried to make friends with them, hoping for the best. They fed me horsemeat and offered me a T-shirt." Thinking his friends had passed by him while he was sleeping, he recommenced kayaking. Then, four days later, a miracle. Mongolian fishermen had spied the film bag in an eddy and retrieved it. "Their being honest guys, they knew that a weirdo plastic bag and a guy coming down the river in a weirdo plastic boat were connected. I was absolutely ecstatic." Besides film, the bag held a paddling jacket and a first-aid kit with some Pepto Bismol. "I was so hungry that the Pepto turned into a delicious treat and every day I'd have my little ration. Such bliss." By now he'd covered about 125 miles and, although fearing starvation, he decided to paddle on to Sukhbaatar, a town on the Mongolian-Russian border 190 miles downstream. He made it but his friends weren't there. Malnourished, without money or passport, Colin finally met some Russians who took pity on him, fed him bread and mutton and put him up in a hotel. To this day, Colin wonders why it took 12 days for his mates to catch up to him.

As planned, a fourth adventurer, Tim Cope, joined the trio in Sukhbaatar. "Tim speaks Russian fluently and translated for us. It made a huge difference. I don't know how many important things the Amazon people told us that we missed because of our lousy Spanish. In Russia we learned amazing things because people would say, 'You've got to see this,' or 'Something interesting is just around the corner.' So we saw a lot that you can't spot from the river."

They changed vessels in Irkutsk. As the raft was awkward to row, they'd planned to find a traditional Russian dory — if it existed — and adapt it. Luckily, an 18-foot boat lay abandoned on the banks. "It was beautifully built, fine craftsmanship with nice planks, but it had gaping holes between the planks. Nobody owned it and we managed a quick patch job by applying layers of fibreglass and waterproofing it with tar." They also bought ply-wood and added a deck and small cabin with sleeping quarters and a galley.

Racing against the coming fall weather, they built a rowing seat and, using long oars, rowed in shifts around the clock. "The rowing is the toughest physically; it just goes on week after week, month after month. With the people and gear, the boat weighed over a ton. In the end we were plagued by the winds coming off the Arctic Ocean, with big waves, making every stroke that much harder." They'd travel for two-week stretches and only stop at villages to buy food. "The people were so generous. Fishermen would throw us some fish, others would bring us vegetables or a pot of berries. And they wanted nothing in return."

When they reached the Arctic, ice was just beginning to film over the river's surface. They'd made it: the four adventurers had achieved what no other group had — a complete descent of the Yenisey. Colin is busy writing another book. In assessing this latest feat, rather than focussing on the sometimes harsh condi-tions, he speaks of the need for a team of adventurers to harmo-nize. "To be compatible with colleagues is essential. Skills can be learned but you can't change character. One of our party, Remy, struck us as arrogant, certainly not co-operative."

"You see," he continues, "when you have four guys in an 18-footer, facing life-and-death decisions, in each other's face 24 hours a day, even a slight problem comes out. In an office, we would probably have been able to tolerate Remy, but on the river, with no escape, he didn't help our enjoyment. Don't get me wrong, I'm not sorry I made the voyage. Even with the human element it was a great learning experience, both positive and negative. Looking back on this Yenisey odyssey, the main thing is that we achieved what we visualized beforehand."

While completing his current book, *Lost in Mongolia,* Colin is busy working out his next adventure. This time it will be solo, without sponsors. "The one that really intrigues me, and may be completely, totally nutty, is to go around the world with absolutely no money, not even for visas and other bureaucracy. There's a cunning side to me that likes being extremely resourceful. Although the more I think about it, the more difficult a trip without money actually becomes." The other quest he's contemplating is a world circumnavigation entirely under his own power. People have walked, jogged, biked and wheelchaired around the world, but always on land, he explains. Someone is rowing around the globe. But nobody has gone around the world on land *and* sea. If Colin chooses this option, he'd cycle up to the Bering Strait, row across, bike through Russia and Europe and then row across the Atlantic. It should only take a couple of years.

After the next trip, he'll go back to the water. He dreams of a converted fish boat that will serve as home and office, where he'll write books with the entire coast as his backyard. "I want to wake up in the morning in some secluded inlet, pull up the crab traps and breakfast on the deck with music playing lightly. I'd work on the computer below and look at the scenery through the portholes. I like rainy, misty days with low clouds and bluish mountains. I'd like to use the energy of the water and the lessons it has taught me. I'd like to harness its flow to my own ends."

Bob Stewart
the hermit

"**P**overty." That's how Bob Stewart explains his hermit lifestyle in a red-painted, floating shack at the edge of Potts Lagoon on West Cracroft Island. "Sheer poverty."

I scrutinize the slim 70-year-old with his youngish face wreathed in Santa Claus hair and beard. The collar of his vivid, tie-dyed shirt is frayed. He's already told me he's itching to buy a wooden schooner. "Really?" I ask a bit skeptically.

Bob's startlingly blue eyes twinkle. "Well," he drawls, "for five years now I've lived on this tiny island, isolated, in ridiculous poverty by Canadian and U.S. standards. Why? So I could pay tuition for my son Josh. He wanted to study the trumpet at a private music college in Seattle." The man who calls himself "Hermit Bob" leans back in his chair. "So I say to myself, 'Hey, forget all the rubbish that went wrong. Never mind. Something finally went right. Josh got his degree.'"

Hermit Bob hasn't always lived away from civilization. He's fathered four children and divorced two wives. For 38 years, he taught math and persuaded youngsters on the verge of failure into more productive paths. And throughout all these years, boats played a primary role.

He once installed a boat in a classroom in a Vancouver suburb. The tale brings a gleam to his eye. "I got this old, 20-foot wooden sailboat up Indian Arm, seven feet wide, with portholes and bunks. But how to get her into the classroom? Well, I sawed the boat into two chunks along one of the planks. I waited for the principal to go home, and with the help of my 30 special-ed kids, we snuck the top and the bottom into the schoolroom. We glued some plywood along the ripped planks and painted it white. It was like putting the boat in a bottle. The kids used to sit in there. Gave them a safe spot. A place to be alone."

He claims his love of boats is genetic. As a child he lived on the water in White Rock, just north of the U.S. border. His father died at 49 of a heart attack — on his boat. His mother then bought her own boat and went around the islands by herself. "To have a really good old age," Bob notes, "you must keep moving and be passionately interested in something. I've been crazy about boats since childhood. I'm mad keen about them." He's designed at least 150 boats and built all manner of them — small power and sailboats, rowboats, dinghies and skiffs, including *Seahunter*, a 23-foot cutter. The biggest he designed was a 42-foot schooner called *Devil Woman* ("a lot of hidden messages there," he grins impishly). He named his son Josh after Joshua Slocum.

"When I had problems and wanted to feel better," he says earnestly, "I'd start designing a boat. Instantly, I don't have to fight with a wife, boss or children. No bills piling up or speeding tickets. I'm in a world that matters. Boat design is challenging intellectually and satisfying emotionally. It has saved my sanity many times. Building them is great too. When you're done, you have a vehicle that's like a magic carpet. You can go somewhere."

He says that, with the advent of the steam engine, the art of sailing is at least 120 years out of date. He also knows that, with the boat market focussing on fibreglass boats with single aluminum masts, stainless rigging and few sails, his love for wooden schooners and scows is outmoded. But that doesn't bother him. A friend of his, Carl Conrad, told him, "When you're looking at a boat to buy, your spirit should soar and your heart should leap or don't bother with the damn thing. It won't be worth the time, money and effort."

"You never get your money out of a boat," Bob continues. "I've lost money on more than 80 boats so far. On the last three, I've beat the bank because I haven't sold them yet. I take losing money for granted. Besides, to me, money isn't very important; it's way down my list."

Keeping Bob in boats did not contribute to his marital happiness. "I have found that almost all women detest boats and struggle against them," he states. "My former brother-in-law once said to my second wife, 'You might have a happier life if you could somehow just accept gracefully that small boats are a part of Bob.' But nooooo … "

After retiring from teaching, Bob spent four years as a boatyard foreman and yacht surveyor, but his second marriage fell apart so, despondent and broke, he went north in his 20-foot sailboat. He first moved into an old shack belonging to another hermit, Mad John, on Harbledown Island with his beloved dog, Phoebe (now deceased), but during the four years he lived in the hut, it mouldered into pieces. Then he found a 730-square-foot float home that rises or plunges 17 feet with the tide on Potts Lagoon, a tidal pond measuring about 1,300 by 1,600 feet. "I bought the whole thing. The shack floats on cabled-together logs and 57 barrels. That gives me about 450 pounds of flotation. The whole thing is hitched to the shore with long cables. I've got about $9,500 into it and it's all paid for. Not exactly cheap by hermit-in-the-woods standards. But compared to Vancouver or Seattle, a real deal. Now I can live on about $10,000 a year." (He clears well over three times that from his pensions.)

The float home, with its sign "Beware of Bob," lacks electricity, running water and telephone. Bob listens to an occasional broadcast on a tiny, battery-run radio, which also plays tapes. A hose from a nearby creek provides water to his shack, but Bob uses rainwater off the roof for his coffee, soup and tooth brushing. "Nature must have distilled it at least once," he says. "I've never had a problem." He takes sponge baths and uses a bucket as a latrine. He cooks on a propane stove. ("I'm real uptown, you see.") He once had a propane fridge, but he gave it away to "two Indians with a sad story." The lack of refrigeration prevents long-term storage of fresh fruits and vegetables, but Bob says he manages. He breakfasts on Fruit Loops and powdered milk, lunches on a bun and coffee, and chews on a radish or two.

Dinner consists of rice, onions, corn, store-bought cake and hot apple juice. Campbell soup is another favourite. Occasionally, he indulges in chicken or turkey. He's got a heart condition and when asked about his need to maintain a balanced diet, he responds simply and philosophically, "I do OK."

Every two weeks he fires up his 18-foot powerboat, *Frog*, with her 90-horsepower Evinrude, and runs the 24.5 miles to Port McNeill where he buys groceries, fills his heart prescriptions, visits the laundromat, eats out with friends, collects his mail, and purchases the hardcover, blank journals he fills with handwritten text.

Bob has written over a hundred books. By hand. The books resemble diaries, crammed with his capital-letter musings. "Often in the morning," he confides, "I'll look around and laugh, Heh! Heh! Heh! and I'll write. Sometimes they're children's stories, an adventure maybe, but even when aimed at children, they're not children's books. They're full of wisdom and philosophy. No stupid things like sex and violence. I don't write spy novels set in Vienna. I write about shacks and the beach and tree forts. My books have a theme, like in *Hamlet*, where you're reading about indecision, or in *Moby Dick* where you're really reading about obsession and compulsion. In my book "Roving Johnny," for example, I told about death. I wrote it for a four-year-old girl whose hamster died. It's a sensitive, tender thing."

Writing is but one occupation filling Bob's days. On a typical day, he rises, takes his medicine, lights a fire in the wood heater, sips a coffee, gazes at the water and the beach ("it's just beautiful"), and begins a new book. Other days, he chainsaws driftwood for his stove, explores islets in his 10.5-foot skiff or putters on his boats.

Bob recalls one visiting yachtsman questioning his isolated lifestyle. He vividly re-enacts the conversation.

"Don't you go stir-crazy?" asked the sailor.

"Not at all."

"My god, how do you combat boredom?"

"I don't know. I've never experienced any yet."

"I don't find the isolation difficult at all," Bob continues. "Almost always I'm alone but almost never do I feel lonely." He sleeps with his teddy bear, Floppy Super Gus, who's been a wonderful buddy since 1973. The longest he's been without seeing another human is 55 days. He thinks of his hut as a little blob of culture in the jungle. "I've got music and books and a lifetime of memories. People visit. And I've never seen so much. Deer, bears, otters, cougars, birds. And wolves. I thought they all looked like skinny German shepherds. But they can be grey, white, pale yellow, black and dark red."

Bob values small boats and likes shallow water. "Mucking around the islands where I live — there's hundreds and hundreds of islands — you could explore them for a lifetime and never see the end of it all. In some ways, this is the best part of my life. I don't feel sorry for myself. If I want to build a tree fort in the jungle by a creek, I will, won't I?"

Now that son Josh has graduated and Bob's no longer broke, he could give up his hermit existence in a semi-wilderness. But he's bought a 1969 wooden schooner and a 16-foot sailing scow. They need some work up at the lagoon. "Boats are what keep me poor now," he growls, eyes sparkling.

Does he worry about his heart condition? Bob knows that choosing to live in his floating home, hours away from medical help and without a telephone, is chancy. His open-heart surgery took place 18 years ago, and he says, "I'm held together with twist ties and stainless staples — I've seen them on X-rays." He takes a slew of meds. But he figures he can last a while by staying fit, lowering his fat intake and reducing stress.

Living alone cuts that stress. "I used to be quite angry," he says. "But I learned I had a choice about being angry. After all, what did it get me? An angry and upset life. One counsellor told me, 'You've been mad at this person since 1939. Do you realize he's been dead for 40 years? You're giving him the power to wreck your life.' I now recognize I can change things. Get a life." That's also why he's willing to take the risk of another heart attack away from medical intervention. "Should I live in the shadow of a hospital in fear, waiting to die? I'd far rather get eaten on some obscure trail, fighting with a bear, than sit and wait, afraid."

Besides, he's grown used to the lifestyle. "I have 160 feet of waterfront and free moorage. Sometimes it's calm and sunny and I mutter, 'Oh dearie me, thank you.'" This is how Hermit Bob poeticizes one of his happy moments in the book he handwrote for his friend Phil Jensen.

Wild Roses
Drunk with the smell of wild roses,
Overcome with passion for the beauty around,
I lie on my back (the summer sun makes this possible),
Stare past the green at the deep deep blue of space
And savour my life for a few moments.

Ron Dick
in the teeth of the wind

At the age of 20, he stared at the tide running out the River Clyde, a vision fuelling his dream to venture out to sea.

At the age of 50, he launched the steel schooner that would fulfil the dream.

At the age of 65, the dream nearly cost him his life.

Ron Dick emerged into the world in 1932 in Glasgow, and although he has lived in Canada for nearly five decades, his lilting brogue still evokes bagpipes and haggis. Even as a child, Ron swam against the current. Unlike the other lads, he spent time at the library (his father called him a "bookworm"); he rowed boats by himself; he didn't smoke or drink; and, most appalling, he cared little about football. He began working in a coal mine at the age of 12. In his later teens, he apprenticed at the Fairfield Shipbuilding & Engineering Company, which built ships of all descriptions. The skills he learned there helped him find his first job at Westinghouse's Hamilton, Ontario, turbine plant after he arrived in Canada on his 21st birthday and, much later, they helped him build his own boat. "I came looking for a better life," Ron says, "and I've surely had one."

One of Hamilton's advantages was its location on Lake Ontario, for travelling by boat had always enthralled the feisty Scot. He vividly recalls a day on the Clyde watching the tide swirl through the pilings while eating his thick, white-bread lunch. "I imagined myself like Huckleberry Finn on an imaginary raft," he writes in his unpublished memoirs, "drifting on that enduring tidal stream to the great adventure and trials that the open sea held for me."

In Hamilton, he conducted "scientific" sailing experiments with bleach bottles, sticks and cardboard sails that showed him that "no matter how much you change the rig, the thing still sails." He added outriggers to a 17-foot canoe, installed a mast and sailed the Trent-Severn Canal system, camping at night. He built a Sunfish out of wood scraps, rigged an old bedsheet and went sailing on a blustery Sunday. Unable to right this glorious vessel after several knockdowns in Hamilton Harbour, he entertained passing ferry passengers by bowing deeply while standing on the keel.

A good 25 years later, Ron started building his boat (not a "yacht," mind you). He'd moved to Kaslo, B.C., on Kootenay Lake with his wife, Marlene, bought a laundromat and fixer-upper buildings he could renovate himself. The idea that had lain "in the dusty corners of my mind" translated itself into a 42-foot steel schooner, a junk-rigged Colvin Gazelle. "It seemed I had no choice in the matter," says Ron, his clear blue eyes sparkling. "I had to build that boat. And it seemed natural I should use steel. [The vessel] was a tool ... a tool I would form and shape with my own hands, that would shelter me from the storms and let me tread the paths of the tradewinds, that would take me on this quest and would, perhaps, fill this want I had."

After "caring for this creature's birth" for three years, he launched *Broomielaw* (named after Glasgow's steamboat quay from which thousands of emigrants left Scotland for Canada, the United States and Australia). With Marlene, he tested his vessel as far north as Alaska. It was not enough — the open ocean beckoned. "You see, it's the sea that fascinates me. The expansiveness of it. Not the places I reach after crossing it. If I just want to go somewhere, I'll go fast on a plane."

In 1984, he made his first solo attempt to sail offshore. Alas, a forestay turnbuckle broke at Race Rocks, a mere five miles from his homeport of Victoria. Judging this a bad omen, he returned to his moorage. His second departure was thwarted by a fierce gale off Cape Flattery at the edge of the Pacific Ocean, and again he turned his bow homewards. But with characteristic mulishness ("I'm not embarrassed to turn back and start over"), he made tracks in his "metal steed" one year later, and this time sailed to Nuku Hiva in French Polynesia's Marquesas in 40 days. It was the beginning of a three-year circumnavigation: he visited Tahiti, Fiji, New Zealand, Australia, South Africa and the Caribbean. On the way he stopped in such attention-grabbing places as St. Helena, to the west of Africa (where Napoleon was kept prisoner until his death in 1821), whose inhabitants were highly welcoming, although the lack of anchorages and wharves made for a short stay. Marlene joined him in St. Maarten and the couple cruised for three months in the balmy West Indies. "Those were good times," grins Ron, "great sailing and rum at $1.99 a bottle." He returned to Vancouver Island through the Panama Canal.

To offset expenses, he took along paying crew — at least, when they were available. He advertised in Canada, but received little response. Later, in New Zealand, his ad brought 40 potential companions, causing Ron to think the Kiwis are more adventurous. Aside from the extra income, Ron took pleasure in having crew aboard. "Our conversations ranged from the mundane to the philosophical; these people felt so free. They knew they'd be aboard for only a bit of time and thus shed their inhibitions. They were truly themselves." He nursed along several severely seasick young people and chuckles relating how one green recruit ("Aye, but he was a dandy!") was impressed by the "thousands of hummingbirds flying the ocean."

"Hummingbirds?" asked Ron. "Where?"

"There, diving into the waves."

"But those are flying fish," roared Ron.

Of all his landfalls, Ron recalls South Africa as one of the most hospitable. He never liked the cold officialdom and indirect bribery demands he encountered in some ports. "The country was still under apartheid," says Ron, "and had few visitors. I was the first offshore boat to arrive that season — they called me the 'mad Scotsman' and plied me with free beer and Scottish meatpies. Never charged for moorage. The only thing they seemed concerned about was the possibility of my having communist literature aboard. Imagine me a communist!" While teaching the "tango to young maidens," he also listened to Afrikaner advice. He sailed from Durban to Cape Town in the fast Agulhas current and had been told that if waterspouts popped up, he should not even think about going on. Waterspouts spring up when the prevailing northeasterlies pushing down Africa's east coast meet the winds coming off the Atlantic from the west, creating tumultuous seas. "Suddenly my compass needle turned circles," says Ron. "I saw spouts and scooted into East London Harbour. There the yacht club was lined with newspaper clippings about ships that have foundered in the spouts. I was happy not to be a hero."

After completing his circumnavigation, Ron's itch next led to a yearlong voyage to Mexico in 1990, but his final — and fateful — bluewater trip started in 1995. "It's as if this voyage had been waiting for me; as if I'd been looking for this challenge." Papua New Guinea beckoned. Ron had rerigged *"Broom"* as a staysail schooner and substituted a GPS for the sextant. With various crew, he stopped in Hawaii and Kiribati, and then passaged to Rabaul, a Papua New Guinean town nearly erased by a volcanic eruption the year before. That's where his traditional distaste for customs officers took an ominous turn: to stay in Papua New Guinea longer than 48 hours, he'd have to obtain a $100 visa. "That didn't sit well with me," says Ron, in one of his rare understatements. He intended to visit Madang, famous for its reefs and World War II sunken ships, so he left Rabaul, hoping for the best. In Madang, he tied up to a jetty, shopped, called home and tried to find the customs office. A tidy-looking young customs official appeared, to whom Ron gave a few cold beers and $35. Ron felt he'd befriended this authoritative-looking fellow and thought he was home free, but the official was a fake. When the real customs officer appeared some days later, the gig was up. Ron tried to understand the official's angry, contradictory statements in pidgin: "You've already exceeded your time limit. While we investigate, you'll be in jail. If you're still here tomorrow, I will arrest you. I strongly suggest you leave. And that's $5 for the paperwork."

Not relishing the idea of languishing in a Papua New Guinean jail, Ron departed within the hour, alone, in mid-September, calculating he'd cover the 6,500 nautical miles to Victoria in about two months. He was convinced he had enough provisions.

The voyage lasted 125 days. Every week a storm or gale lasting three days would hit. "It'd pass," he recalls, "then turn around and bite me in the ass." His sails blew out one by one. He stitched them time and again on his hand-cranked sewing machine until he ran out of thread. He made a sea anchor combining plywood and a 30-pound, four-pronged Swedish rock anchor and deployed it. "It was a work of art, but it didn't do a damn bit of good," he says with a typical wry turn of phrase. He had enough battery power to run the GPS, but turned off the VHF to save precious juice. The portholes leaked. He rarely lit the diesel heater in hopes of hoarding his scarce fuel for motoring into Juan de Fuca Strait. Instead, he dried his clothes on a colander over the oil lamp. When he grew concerned about running out of propane, he soaked his oats, rice and pasta to shorten cooking time. One by one, he ran out of staples and coffee. "As it was really important for me to have a hot drink, I reused my teabags many times. One of my crew had left behind a good supply of spices, so I invented such unusual drinks as ginger tea and Tabasco cocktail. I lost 50 pounds. I gave thought to dying, but I didn't want to perish in that cold, wet world. I knew eventually I'd reach the coast, but would I be alive?" In these extreme times, his head "flew all over the place." At one point, he thought his father was travelling at his side, making him reflect on the continuity of life. Although both his parents died young, Ron felt their energy lodged inside him, helping him carry on. Refusing to surrender, he finally limped into port on January 15, 1996, jury-rigged and two months overdue, into Marlene's waiting arms. It was his last bluewater voyage. *Broomielaw* was sold.

"But," Ron muses six years later, "I wouldn't have missed it for the world. It's as if the experience and the sea had been waiting for me, as if I'd been programmed. Call it fate, or destiny. Tears creep into my eyes when I think about it. I've heard whales breathe and seen a billion purple-tinted sail jellies float by. Although I'm not religious, the voyage made me more spiritual. I wanted to be in the middle of the ocean, the only time I feel completely whole. The trivialities of land, of politics, religion and family fade. Only one thing matters: survival. Sometimes I felt like a god — not because I am a god, but because I was fortunate enough to be on the sea and feel the purity of reality."

Sven Johansson
salt of all trades

Seven summers. That's what it took for Sven Johansson to skipper the 60-foot *Belvedere* through the ice-laden Northwest Passage from the Pacific to the Atlantic. The saga began in early 1982 after John Bockstoce, a Massachusetts-based risk-taker with a love for the Arctic, recruited Sven, an adventurous ship's captain, reindeer specialist and bush pilot. Bockstoce wanted to be on the first yacht to cross the Northwest Passage from west to east and sought a skipper who knew ice.

Intrigued by the challenge, Sven left for San Diego to locate the right boat. "I found a 60-foot, twin-keeled, three-quarter-inch steel cutter called *Pacifier*. Obviously, we couldn't cross the Arctic Ocean in a boat sucking her thumb," the Swedish-born adventurer chuckles. "We renamed her *Belvedere*, after the famous whaler. She'd just come in from Hawaii and drew only five feet. I had the keels cut off and then rewelded with a weak weld. You see, when the ice buckles between the keels, it can rip them off and shatter the boat. I wanted the keels to shear off easily."

Later that year, Sven brought *Belvedere* to Victoria and refurbished her for Arctic duty. He added a pilot house, insulated her to avoid condensation, dismantled the air-conditioning system and put in four heating systems: a glycol-laced hot-water system, a diesel heater, separate diesel stove and a wood-burning stove that could also burn seal blubber.

In early May the following year, Sven and his crew set sail for New York through the Northwest Passage. Although rough weather was still a threat, he timed their departure to benefit from the following winds that blew the yacht to Dutch Harbor in the Aleutians. There they waited until the Pacific high kicked in, the Bering Strait ice melted and they could sail on to Point Barrow, the northernmost tip of Alaska. Travel north of the Bering Strait cannot begin until early August, and then only if the winds are southerly, blowing the ice north; easterlies push the ice onto the beaches. "For ships in the far north, timing is everything." *Belvedere* made it through the Beaufort Sea, arriving in Tuktoyaktuk on August 26, too late in the season to transit the Northwest Passage's closing ice fields.

For the next five summers, the team tried to outwit the weather, leaving Tuktoyaktuk in late July after the Beaufort Sea's frozen vastness thawed sufficiently for a yacht to squeak through. They'd thread their way through the slob ice as fast as possible, but each year, new pack ice would threaten to crush or trap the vessel and force a return to Tuktoyaktuk. "We'd spend from three to five weeks wending our way between icebergs and sheets. But if we hit ice, it was on purpose." Sometimes Sven would deliberately steer the boat into a crack and then try to crash through the rest of the sheet, transforming the vessel into a mini-icebreaker.

In 1987, they again left Mackenzie Bay and came within 300 miles of their target — the Atlantic — before blockading ice floes forced them to return. "The following year, we thought we'd lost again. Heaps of ice piled up around us, grinding against the hull. We crept along and then anchored for four days until an east wind shifted the ice enough to let us sneak through and reach Baffin Bay, and later, Holsteinsborg in Greenland." The boat was put on the hard and the following summer, after sailing to Godthaab (now Nuuk), they journeyed south through Davis Strait toward Labrador. "The wind and weather co-operated in early July," says Sven, "although we still had to transit ice packs." They anchored off Cartwright, a small community in Labrador, located inside a protected fjord, where the temperatures soared. "We couldn't fathom it," says Sven. "We went from freezing to

100°. I'm talking Fahrenheit, of course." After stopping in Nova Scotia, *Belvedere* reached New York to great fanfare.

Sven seems to have danced through life, which may account for his ageless look. He's short and roly-poly, with still-tawny hair and a handshake that crushes my bones. One of his mottos for living a meaningful life is "Never a bad day." He dropped out of school after Grade 6 and claims the overflowing floor-to-ceiling bookcases lining the walls of his bachelor apartment and the stacks of music CDs ranging from Bach to jazz constitute his formal education. "Had to make up for it, you know."

Although he spent half his life on the water, Sven never took formal ship handling or navigation training. Born west of Stockholm in Seffle, Sweden, 78 years ago, this man of many talents learned on the job. When he was six, his family moved near Göteborg, on Sweden's west coast, where "every damn kid builds a raft." Later, when he was 20, he sailed a friend's small boat whenever he could. "It gave me a good sense of the wind and water and helped me become a serious boating professional."

After World War II, he moved north to Lapland, "living in the wilderness, which I loved." He got to know and work with local reindeer herders and spent winters hunting, fishing and trapping. In his late 20s, he landed a summers-only captain's job on a 36-foot diesel boat transporting freight across a chain of lakes in Northern Sweden. They'd portage goods by hand-pushing railroad carts on narrow-gauge tracks linking the lakes. A locomotive powered by a car engine would sometimes push the heavier loads, if, Sven laughs, they could get hold of the key to the loco shed. "Our boat carried whole trucks hanging over the bow — there wasn't much regulation in that remote part. Sometimes I'd be so sleep-deprived I'd see things that weren't there — terrific homework for transiting the Northwest Passage. Nonstop training. But I never had an accident. And I had great fun."

He opted to leave Sweden when the government published plans to build hydropower plants in the wilderness and change the inhabitants' way of life. Searching for other wild places, he singled out Arctic Canada as the logical choice, and his experience with reindeer helped him immigrate to Canada. "It's easy to become an expert in such a narrow field," Sven comments in his singsong Swedish accent. "I wanted to leave Sweden. They wanted someone to take charge of the Canadian Reindeer Project. I ended up in Inuvik on the Mackenzie River delta with the task of turning around the reindeer industry — food for the Inuit when caribou herds were scarce."

Hired as an independent contractor, Sven arrived at Reindeer Station on the Mackenzie south of Tuktoyaktuk. The project was in trouble because the Inuit approach to reindeer herding differed greatly from the directives sent by Ottawa. "The bureaucrats wanted intensive, close-in herding," says Sven. "But large herds need extensive grazing areas. These animals must roam freely and widely to find scarce tundra plants. So that's what we let them do." Sven reorganized the herds, corralled the animals only when it was needed and calmed the discord. "We patrolled the range against predators, both four- and two-footed ones." In five years, he made reindeer herding a viable industry — and when local demand for reindeer meat was low, he froze the surplus and shipped it south. Sometimes that involved boats. "To transport the meat, we used canoes with outboards, barges and tugs," he says, a gleam in his eye. "Then we located *Nanuk*, a heavy wooden government ship with planks missing and no engine." Sven and Inuit friends repaired it and installed an engine. "It worked great. These people were incredibly technically skilled."

With the reindeer organized, Sven, always entrepreneurial, trapped fox and ptarmigan for four years in the Mackenzie Mountains, built a cabin, hunted for food and became a big-game outfitter, guiding clients in August and September, the two months before the snow falls. As the nearest neighbour was 100 miles away, he bought a plane, attached fat, spongy "tundra tires" so he could land on rocks and bumps, and earned his pilot's licence. Although it was isolated, he loved his life in the mountains. "You have complete independence, you know. It's a rich, interesting life."

In 1967, Sven fell in love — with the *North Star of Herschel Island*. The last of the western Arctic cargo ships, she had been built for two Inuit fox trappers in 1935 at the George W. Kneass Shipyard in San Francisco. The 57-foot sloop transported furs and supplies from Aklavik and Tuktoyaktuk to Sachs Harbour on Banks Island. "They'd trap white fox," says Sven. "But they had to have their own water transport — dog teams could only carry small loads and the animals needed too much feed." Usually, the *North Star* was beached during the long gloomy winter, and when her services became superfluous after airplanes began transporting cargo in the Arctic in the early 1960s, she remained abandoned on a Banks Island beach for six years. Her clipper-ship–shaped hull and her charm captured Sven's heart. That, and the planked inner hull covered with Irish ship's felt overlain with Australian greenheart, an exceptionally dense hardwood also used to sheathe Shackleton's *Endurance*. "The *North Star* was a ship that could freeze and survive," Sven says. "And she had sails. That saves on fuel."

He bought her and began repairs in Inuvik. "I had no plans for the boat and said to myself, 'What will you do with her?'" Nonetheless, he installed a new diesel engine and refitted her for use in the Beaufort Sea. One day, two Calgarians shouting at him from the shore solved his dilemma: oil had been found in Alaska's Prudhoe Bay and the Canadian oil patch was prospecting in the Northwest Territories. "That first charter with those Calgarians in the Beaufort Sea paid for making the boat seaworthy and left me with money to spare. I was lucky. There weren't any other boats in the delta. Later, I even became a supply ship for a Houston oil company." He was also hired by the Geological Survey of Canada, which was studying the region's flora, fauna, sea-bottom conditions and permafrost composition for potential pipelines. He assisted with research studies on oil-feeding bacteria. "These microbes are a natural way of curing oil spills," says Sven. "There are only a few around naturally, but when oil enters the water, these critters multiply like crazy." His gamble on the old ship had paid off and the *North Star* became his home for nearly three decades.

"I took enormous pride in never putting a scratch on either the *North Star* or *Belvedere*," continues Sven. "I was always cautious and knew I'd survive. That's called seamanship." He'd read in a *National Geographic* about David Lewis's voyage single-handing through the Antarctic in his 32-foot sloop, *Ice Bird*. Lewis had been quoted as saying, "The voyage seemed a sure rendezvous with death." Sven finds himself at crosscurrents with that sentiment. "I never believed in that attitude," he says. "When you undertake these adventures, you must have a pleasant time. And you must make your decisions *before* you get icebound."

In the early 1970s, Sven, married with a young daughter, decided to move south. He had observed changes in Arctic Canada, changes he didn't endorse. "The Inuit had been independent for thousands of years," he says. "But do-gooders from the south who knew nothing about their way of life persuaded the government the aboriginals had been badly treated, that they'd been victimized. The government listened, tried to make Inuit into middle-class folks, but created dependence instead. I didn't want to stay." The family sailed aboard the *North Star* through the Bering Strait and arrived in Vancouver by 1974. A year later, Sven had settled at Victoria's Fisherman's Wharf as a live-aboard. In summer, his boat supplied the International Boundary Commission surveying the B.C. and Alaska coasts; in winter, he offered sail training to young people. Often, he'd moor the boat at a dock somewhere between Sooke and Courtenay, and school classes would visit the ship. "I used the ship as an introduction to seamanship and life skills. We'd tie knots. I'd focus on teamwork, like hoisting the teacher while singing a shanty. It taught responsibility for someone's life."

He also converted the *North Star* into a three-masted schooner, adding a bowsprit and jib boom, and making her the only fully square-rigged sailing ship in Canada, carrying 16 sails, including royals.

During his many adventures, Sven never worried about money. "I've always disregarded money. That's why I can do so many things. I don't let the lack of it stop me. I jump in headlong and the money comes. Money is a resource you must use immediately to make life better. Don't keep it — it does nothing for you."

In 1993, Sven was made a companion of the Order of Canada, an honour that recognizes lifetime achievement. The award acknowledged Sven's contributions to wildlife management and reindeer husbandry, and his key role in navigating the first private vessel through the Northwest Passage.

His life on the water and in the wild didn't foreshadow Sven's most recent — and most dramatic — career change. He sold the *North Star* in 1996 to pursue his other passion: dance. Convinced that dance is limited by gravity, he invented mechanical instruments that support dancers through the entire space on a stage, allowing even disabled people to dance. Sven choreographs works and takes performers to Europe, and his work has been televised.

How does living with the elements for most of his life fit with dance? "The sea taught me to be humble," Sven said fervently. "I always wanted to learn what the sea is about — its force, its way. Then you learn not to do things against the sea but to be harmonious with it. This respect for the sea's power shapes your character so you can adapt to anything in life."

He sometimes misses the ocean but has no regrets. "'Never look back' is my motto. It gives you a kink in the neck."

Jim Whittaker
into thick air

When tall, trim Jim Whittaker strides down Port Townsend's waterfront, his clothes shout his approach to life. Heavy black letters on his white cotton T-shirt read, "INDOOR BAD." Turn him around and the slogan on his back proclaims, "OUTDOOR GOOD."

Jim has lived — and still lives — that philosophy. One of the first things the hazel-eyed 73-year-old tells me aboard his 54-foot steel ketch, *Impossible*, is that he's promised to take his two teenaged sons up Mount Rainier before too long. He's already taken them sailing for four years through the South Pacific as far as Australia. By scaling the glaciers of Mount Rainier with them he will have handed down two of his life passions: mountaineering and sailing.

Both water and mountain climbing permeated Jim's youth. He was born in Seattle, where his mother frequently took him, his identical twin, Louie, and older brother, Barney, to the beach. As the boys grew older, they lashed together log rafts and spent countless hours splashing about Puget Sound. One day, they found a small, broken-up sailboat on the beach, hauled it home and with their father's help, repaired it, installed a dagger board and sailed. They'd fish for perch and cod. "That's how I learned about the water," says Jim. "Just enjoying trailing my hand in the water, looking at the fish, setting the sails or drifting in a rowboat."

At the age of 12, the twins joined the Boy Scouts. Boyhood excursions and family holidays had already taught them to enjoy the wild, but, says Jim, "scouting taught me to live in it and develop an outdoor ethic." Two years of scouting later, the teens met mountaineers Tom Campbell and Lloyd Anderson, who changed their lives forever.

Mountain climbing became an obsession for Jim — eventually leading him to a career and fame. His outdoor conditioning made him a natural climber. Starting in the Cascades, then graduating to the Olympics, he climbed ever more demanding slopes. At the age of 20, an overconfident ascent left him within split seconds of falling and dying — a terrifying memory still as immediate as if it happened yesterday, and an experience that he believes made him into an "extraordinarily careful climber." By 1950, both Jim and Louie had become guides on Mount Rainier, a job that spawned a company called Rainier Mountaineering, which became a lifelong occupation for Louie. Along the way, they received basketball scholarships to Seattle University. Jim, in keeping with his love of the natural world, majored in biology. After army service (where he trained "Special Forces soldiers in skiing, climbing, mountain manoeuvres and bivouacs"), and the birth of the first of his and his wife Blanche's three sons, he hopped aboard the fledgling "Co-op," an outfit where mountaineers could buy good climbing equipment at reasonable cost. It became a career lasting 25 years. Today, Recreational Equipment International (REI) is a billion-dollar company.

Although REI grew strongly, Jim never quit climbing. He roped up for ever taller mountains, including Alaska's Mount McKinley which, at 20,300 feet, is North America's highest peak. In 1962, he was invited to join an American expedition to climb Mount Everest and was put in charge of preparing the gear and supplies for this monumental trek. The climb, sponsored by the National Geographic Society, was accompanied by almost 1,000 porters, and suffered bad weather, Arctic temperatures and the devastating death of one of the climbers, Jake Breitenbach. Nevertheless, after two years of planning and two months of climbing, on May 1, 1963, Jim and his Sherpa guide, Gombu, breathlessly reached the highest point on earth, 29,028 feet above sea level. Jim was the first American to achieve this feat.

A hero's welcome awaited him after returning home. In July, just four months before Dallas, President John F. Kennedy presented Jim and the other expedition members with the National Geographic Society's Hubbard Medal. Two years later, the Canadian government named the highest unclimbed peak in the Yukon's St. Elias Mountains in honour of the assassinated president. Because of Jim's Everest experience, he was asked to lead a surveying expedition up the 14,000-foot, glacier-covered mountain. One of the team members was Senator Robert Kennedy, who, although inexperienced in mountain climbing, became the first person to reach the summit of the mountain named after his brother. The gruelling climb led to a close friendship between the senator and Jim, who was introduced to the life of the rich and powerful in the east. Jim frequently sailed on Teddy Kennedy's yacht and even visited Aristotle and Jackie Onassis on their 365-foot powerboat. Spending time at Robert and Ethel Kennedy's home, he soaked up the intense political atmosphere and eventually took on the job of organizing the Washington State "Kennedy for President" campaign in 1968. Shortly afterwards, he served as a pallbearer at Bobby's funeral.

A busy business life, weekends spent climbing, politics, travelling and a slow "growing apart" cost Jim his marriage to Blanche. He buried himself in work and worried about his sons. Then he met Canadian photographer Dianne Roberts. Although Jim is two decades her senior, they fell in love and married. Dianne learned to climb and has scaled Mount Rainier a dozen times. That's why, in 1973, the couple accepted an invitation to organize and lead an expedition to climb K2 which, at 28,250 feet, is the world's second-highest mountain; it straddles the border between China and Pakistan. The first attempt to ascend this mountain failed due to snafus, bad weather, illness, avalanches and disagreements with porters. Fortunately, another team led by a stubborn Jim succeeded three years later.

During the K2 climb, Dianne took along a book on offshore sailing. "She learned all the words," says Jim, "the arcane terminology — shackles, sheets and so forth — so everyone thought she was a really experienced sailor. But she'd never sailed." Nevertheless, the couple was smitten with the idea of sailing and, after getting off the mountain, bought a Fuji 35. They named the yacht *Impossible* and participated in a Swiftsure race — a miserable, cold, wet, high-wind, overnight event that made Jim dreadfully seasick. But they were hooked on racing, so when a friend wanted to film the Victoria-Maui race, Jim, who'd retired from the presidency of REI, agreed enthusiastically. "*Impossible* was an old Japanese cruising cutter with a long keel, definitely not a lightweight performance cruiser, but we outfitted her with a spinnaker. Soon I felt as comfortable on the high seas as I did on the high summits." Accompanied by a crew of four, Jim and Dianne took well over three weeks to sail to Maui, arriving in bouncy Lahaina Harbor with 13 glass floats tied to the back of the yacht. They were dead last but slid spiritedly into port sporting a banner that read, "The Impossible Takes a Little Longer."

Three years later, in 1979, Jim graduated to a 44-foot Swan cutter which, in his view, is the "Stradivarius of sailboats." He entered other Swiftsures. In the summers, he and Dianne explored Desolation Sound. "We stayed in some places that nobody knows. Little coves, where I'd climb up and hammer pitons into the rocks above and we'd be safely anchored in 400 feet of water. This is where mountaineering and sailing merged."

Having grown confident on his Swan, the second *Impossible*, he was determined not to be last in his next Vic-Maui race, which he and a crew of seven, including his 16-year-old son Bobby, undertook in 1982. It took only 17 days. After the strenuous race, they left on holiday, continuing to sail in 25-knot beam winds toward the Big Island, and Jim found out that sailing can be as dangerous as mountain climbing. In the middle of the Alenuihaha Channel, their 70-foot mast cracked, covering Dianne with a tangle of rigging, halyards, sheets and sails. Fortunately, she was unhurt, and Jim, grabbing bolt-cutters and hacksaws, severed the shrouds holding pieces of the mast, the mainsail and jib. A small, frozen, ball-and-socket attachment on the rod rigging had led to this catastrophic failure. The device's non-performance caused such stress on the leeward shroud that it sheared off and brought down the now-unsupported mast.

Jim and Dianne had two sons in the early 1980s. They moved from busy downtown Seattle to Port Townsend, with its sedate traffic and clean air, and began building a spectacular log home that one of their friends nicknamed the "Log Mahal." Life was good.

But a second mast was about to splinter — one without insurance to cover the damage. Several years earlier, Jim had formed a partnership with businessman Jim O'Malley to manufacture outdoor clothing. Jim became the company's chair, while O'Malley served as CEO. The business did well, but one day the bank called the partners in to discuss their line of credit. To his horror, Jim learned O'Malley had significantly overstated the accounts receivable and the company was deeply in debt. As a full partner, Jim was personally liable and owed nearly a million dollars.

Jim and Dianne mortgaged the house, sold the boat and other assets, and spent the next years trying to recover emotionally and re-establish themselves financially. Although O'Malley's fraud dented Jim's confidence in others, he wrote in his 1999 autobiography, "You can go through life protecting yourself at every turn from disappointment and risk, and as a result, lead a safe, if uneventful, life in which you never have to trust your fellow man. Or you can lead an 'undefended life,' a life on the edge in which you marvel at the general goodness of people and, occasionally, get hurt. I chose the latter course."

His belief in goodness has been confirmed. While still in the doldrums, he was offered the chairmanship of a company developing a device that would tell people instantly where they were: a hand-held, satellite-linked global positioning unit designed for sailors, hikers, climbers and anyone needing to know their location. It was the now-ubiquitous GPS. The company's name? Magellan.

Other adventures surfaced. Jim led the 1990 Peace Climb, an expedition to place representatives of the U.S., China and the Soviet Union on top of Mount Everest. Getting the three traditional enemies and cultural rivals to co-operate was an arduous and time-consuming diplomatic undertaking, but once it was agreed to, Jim added another target. Recognizing that the climb would coincide with the 20th anniversary of Earth Day, he capitalized on a concept developed at REI, which has become a universal slogan, "Pack it in, pack it out." The team carried out tons of trash at the end of the expedition: the first, but not the last, to begin cleaning up the mountain.

In 1994, Jim realized he and Dianne were working too hard to maintain house and hearth — work that limited time with family. So they sold the large house and purchased a third yacht they again christened *Impossible*. Jim had been eyeing the steel ketch (he's actually able to stand up in her) and bought her after a December storm lifted the vessel, her float and all her neighbours above the piers in North Puget Sound. "The whole marina with the boats still tied on floated into shore," Jim recalls with a laugh. "This steel boat sank five beautiful fibreglass hulls. They called her Ms. Pacman. I figured she'd be able to withstand reefs and floating debris."

That fall, after decades of outdoor adventures into thin air, Jim invited Dianne and Joss, 13, and Leif, 11, to stay firmly in an oxygenated environment by sailing south along the coast to Mexico. From there, they set out for the Marquesas and the Tuamotus, their first South Pacific islands. "The plan was to sail around the world in three years, but we found it's a big world at seven knots." They also got into the rhythms of the yachting life and learned it was hard to leave some of the glorious places they visited. They stayed in the Pacific.

Not everything was beautiful. Sensitive to environmental issues, Jim strongly disliked American Samoa and its debris-filled harbour. "It was a hell of a mess — I counted 21 half-submerged plastic shopping bags off the boat's bow one morning. It was just a disgrace. So we had a clean-up one day with the other yachties. Collected all the plastic bottles and bags. Once their society used leaves and other biodegradable stuff, but plastic lasts forever."

In Fiji, Jim watched three circular cloud formations — hurricanes — drift down, but the boat escaped damage. Jim, who continually compares mountaineering and sailing, thinks mountaineering may occasionally be safer — at least during storms.

"In the mountains, you can crawl into a snow or ice cave where it's still and you can't even hear the screeching winds. But the boat's moving all the time. Both fishermen and mountain people have great respect for nature because they love it, and with love comes respect. It's a common saying that there are no atheists in foxholes. Let me add there are no atheists among long-distance cruisers either. I say mountain climbers rope up so the smart ones can't leave, and I say ocean cruisers are too far from land for the smart ones to swim to shore."

After four years on the water, Jim decided the boys needed more than home schooling, although his sons, now teenagers, "read, navigated, worked the radios and sails, scuba dived, and met people of all kinds, sitting on dirt floors and playing their own drums. They knew how to take care of the boat and had learned to be self-sufficient." The family returned to Port Townsend. Fortunately, the boys were ahead of their class — Joss is off to Brown University and Leif is completing high school. The Mountaineers Books published Jim's autobiography and he now spends part of his time as a motivational speaker "to get people out in nature." He's become the spokesperson for a new on-line company, Altrec, promoting the outdoors through the sale of high-quality outdoor equipment and clothing. He's involved with setting up the Northwest Maritime Center, which will teach people about "the magic of the sea." "After all," says Jim with characteristic fervour, "who's going to vote for a clean Puget Sound if they're not out there paddling around, self-propelled? They'll take care of it only if they love it and respect it."

Jim still ardently supports the Boy Scouts that started him on his adventures in the wild. "Their creed says it all," he says. "'On my honor I'll do my best to do my duty to God and my country, to obey the scout law, to help other people at all times and to keep myself physically strong and mentally awake and morally straight.' There it is, laid out right there. What could be better?"

He also emphasizes the interconnectedness of the physical world. "The water we are floating on now has come off the summit of Mount Everest, the highest point on earth. The glaciers melt into rivers and the rivers flow into the sea. I walked on

3,000 to 4,000 feet of ice, a form of water that gravity has pulled down; we're floating in it now. This is the connection from the highest mountain peak on the globe, where nothing lives, down to the sea, where all of us live. It's a magical planet.

"The toughest experiences turn out to be the most fun; the hardest things you do give you the greatest feeling of satisfaction. So when you do things out there on the edge, you grow confident. Nature offers the greatest challenges; nature is a teacher. Sure, there are objective dangers outside your control. You know if that slope gets another foot of snow, it will avalanche, and that the thunderheads kissing the ocean may lead to lightning. But if you're not living on the edge, you're taking up too much space."

the sea
as muse

Edith Iglauer
rampant curiosity

Edith Iglauer is not an easy person to interview. While she graciously welcomes me into her home on Garden Bay in north Pender Harbour, her more-than-60 years of journalistic investigation compel her to ask, rather than answer, questions. With laser-beam inquisitiveness she asks me the who, what, when and how. Repeatedly, I remind her she's the subject — not I. It's evident Edith has been blessed with "rampant curiosity," as her second son, Richard Hamburger, describes her thirst for knowing. That passion also underpins her incisive *New Yorker* articles on air pollution, the World Trade Center's foundations and Pierre Trudeau, as well as books on Inuit co-operatives, an ice road in the Northwest Territories, Canadian architect Arthur Erickson and *Fishing with John*, the bestseller narrating her love for John Daly and their life together on the sea.

Edith lives in the brown-planked, yellow-trimmed house she shared with John until his death in the late 1970s. From the dock, with its small runabout ready to tour the bay, it's a steep walk up a path fringed by pink sweet peas and a handrail of rebar painted green. Edith greets me on the broad deck lined with potted roses, violets, geraniums, basil and rosemary. She's a handsome, diminutive woman, outfitted elegantly in white linen slacks, a soft blue blouse, matching ceramic necklace and dangly silver earrings. She frequently puts on and removes glasses whose frames resemble Joseph's coat of many colours. Her hair is a white aureole, although her trademark eyebrows are still black. She talks to me about her on-deck herb and flower garden, then points to a deep, claw-footed bathtub on the deck. Copper tubing sticks through the wooden slats leading to the bright brass faucets; red geraniums encircle the tub. She flashes a mischievous smile. "That's where I can bathe *au naturel*."

We talk in her spacious kitchen, and although Edith has installed some modern appliances, the kitchen displays the practical touches a fisherman accustomed to ocean swells might add. Next to the hefty, old-fashioned cooking stove, canted shelves clutch a series of different-sized pot lids. Hooks clasp a collection of pans. Groups of cabinets line the walls. Next to the kitchen, a narrow living room is clad in coffee-coloured, diamond-patterned spruce, with a long, sagging shelf crammed with an eclectic selection of books running the length of one wall. Well-used furniture, heirlooms, bits of china and paintings make the room cozy, a place to call home. In the hallway, more hand-built bookshelves occupy every bit of vertical space between doors.

Edith began life 85 years ago in Cleveland, Ohio. At Wellesley College, she read Lincoln Steffens' autobiography describing his relentless investigations of municipal corruption and vowed to pursue the same career. After graduating, she parked herself every day outside the offices of Cleveland's three daily newspaper editors, giving two hours to each newshound. She came to be recognized by every newspaper employee, but it didn't result in a job; thus, that fall, she enrolled at Columbia's Graduate School of Journalism and began writing freelance articles. During World War II, she prepared radio broadcasts for the Office of War Information and covered Eleanor Roosevelt's weekly press conferences. Toward the end of that conflict, Edith joined her then husband, *New Yorker* war correspondent Philip Hamburger, and sent dispatches to the *Cleveland News* from Yugoslavia ("everything was rationed, food ... medicine, clothing, and freedom").

Her lucid, well-researched writings led to assignments for *Harper's, Atlantic Monthly* and, eventually, *The New Yorker*. Because she freelanced, her career allowed her enough time to raise two sons, Jay and Richard. Sometimes she chose article topics — such as the one on New York City's mounted police — that allowed her to take the boys along. But when her marriage failed, her New York life lost its sheen as well. "I found it very tough in New York after my divorce. When I wrote stories about Canada's far north and the Inuit co-operatives, I met many people who said that if I liked the Arctic, I'd like British Columbia even more. So in 1969, I rented a station wagon, and with my boys, three air mattresses and some sleeping bags, I set out to visit B.C. No one told us we'd need a tent for West Coast deluges, so we spent a lot of time sleeping in that station wagon. A wonderful trip. We camped all over Vancouver Island and I fell in love with B.C."

One place she visited was Simon Fraser University in a Vancouver suburb. Dazzled by the architecture, Edith tucked away the architect's name — Arthur Erickson — for future reference and returned to New York. Then in 1973, her friend, the author Paul St. Pierre, offered to rent her his Vancouver apartment. She crossed the continent again with a *New Yorker* assignment on Erickson in hand, a task that provided a superb entrée into Vancouver's creative community. Shortly afterwards, she met John Daly, a commercial fisherman, who had spent as many years catching spring salmon as Edith had writing. He told her he felt at one with the sea and the mountains and was part of the B.C. coast. She fell in love with his outdoor vision and with him, and for the next five fishing seasons shared John's life on the *MoreKelp*, his 41-foot troller. During the winters, they lived in Pender Harbour.

How can a sophisticated city dweller, accustomed to a life rich with artists, writers and musicians, go fishing for months on a boat without a head? "I just loved John," Edith says simply. She also believes her childhood experiences prepared her to adapt to changing circumstances. "My father had a cabin in the country. When I was growing up, we'd go out there on Sundays. My mother loved my father so she put up with the terrible cabin and its outhouse and no running water. We washed our plates in the stream. That stayed with me. When I went to the Arctic, people asked how I could do something so different, but I was just following in my father's footsteps. I'd been taught never to complain ... I loved the whole business of using kerosene stoves and eating dried food. I was able to wash dishes in less water than anybody. So later, life on John's boat was an extension of that early training."

While serving tea in delicate china accompanied by homemade blueberry cake, Edith tells me how John and the boat changed her life and her values. Spending fishing seasons on the narrow *MoreKelp*, she learned nautical and fishing terminology — a language of its own. She discovered binnacles and wildly coloured plastic lures, trolling rigs and gurdies, and learned that many folk valued red salmon more than white. She found that John's height, six feet four inches, allowed him to clamber aboard the *MoreKelp* with ease, while hoisting her five-foot two-inch frame above the freeboard from a dinghy was a life-threatening exercise. Using the VHF radio for the first time turned into a sweat-provoking experience. She found out that a vinegar-water solution combined with a scrubber made from newspapers cleaned the boat's pilot house windows better than Windex. She created an "ergonomic" writing place on John's bunk using pillows, folded long underwear, a blanket, a floater jacket and a hard dishpan as back support so she could tap on the typewriter perched on a board.

She caught a few fish and cleaned them, but never took to killing fish. Only slowly did she reconcile herself to what she called "death in the cockpit." Not liking the destruction of living things, yet knowing people need to eat, she told John one day, "I have accepted your philosophy. I have accepted my place in the food chain to which every living creature belongs."

Although Edith cherished her time with John on the *MoreKelp*, along with the salty air, sunsets and the beauty of the B.C. coast, running the boat did not come naturally. "I'm not safe steering a fishing boat by myself," she says. "I wish I'd started on the water earlier." She recalls how a visitor once saw her prowl around the vessel. "'Edith,' he said, 'don't ever let go of one thing until you're holding onto another.' Best piece of advice I ever got." She adds that John reminded her often that the "sea is out to get you and don't you forget it."

John also taught her to put things back in their place. "I didn't do that when I first got on the boat," she chuckles. "I put tools, pots and cups down where I happened to drop them. He told me we could drown if things were in the wrong place in an emergency. It's a habit now. I still put things back."

What she most enjoyed about the fishing life was getting to know the coastal people who earn their living from the sea. "I don't think appearances matter much anymore. I began to see that when I wrote about Inuit co-operatives in the Arctic. But until I came to British Columbia I'd never known people who could do things like build houses. I'd grown up to be professional and to be around professionals ... I was a snob. I'd never been with fishermen. I learned they were the most wonderful people in the world. I found that people who work with their hands, who keep going no matter what, are marvellous. I prefer them most of the time."

During the fishing seasons, Edith continued to write, completing the Erickson profile, which later became a book. "John wasn't interested in architecture the way I am," she says, "but he was a good listener and critic." While learning how much a fisherman needs to know — navigation, meteorology, tides and currents, mechanical skill, boat handling, fishing and, of course, handling fish properly until they're delivered — she began taking notes on the intricacies of a fishing career. Along the way, she and John married. She still titters at the memory of his purchase of a sky-blue, wooden toilet seat for the beat-up galvanized pail that served as the onboard head. That seat was part of his marriage proposal.

A heart attack took John's life in 1978 at a dance in The Pas, Manitoba, where the couple had gone to visit John's son, Sean. Two years later, Edith began composing *Fishing with John*, which many readers regard as a love story. It is, on many levels: the love of a man and a woman for each other, a love of the fishing life, a deep appreciation of the sea, an everlasting delight in the British Columbia coast, a love of life. The book was nominated for a Governor General's Award. "I spent eight years writing it. I was so desperate without him. So I went into my room and lived with him while I wrote it. He's still very much a part of me."

She also made B.C. her permanent home. As she wrote in *Fishing*, "with the new pair of eyes that John had given me, I could not go back to what I had been before." She added a modern office to the house, where a screen plastered with faded *New Yorker* covers and the framed original drawings illustrating her articles recall her earlier life. A few years ago she met former logger Frank White, who offers "wonderful companionship."

She's active in many Pender Harbour community activities, still writes short pieces and compiled *The Strangers Next Door*, a compendium of her work. Her phone rang continuously after the September 11 terrorist attack, when journalists from around the world asked for her insights on the Trade Center towers' foundations. Thirty years ago *The New Yorker* published her seven-year study describing the monumental effort of digging, reinforcing and waterproofing the 10-storey-deep foundations, sometimes called the "Big Bathtub."

Edith looks back over her long life with composure. "I didn't actually feel at all old until people got up and let me have their seats on buses," she says in her deep voice. Her health is good, although cataract operations two years ago added some unwanted clarity. "I looked in the mirror and asked myself, 'Who is this person with these lines in her face?' I thought I was the only woman to have reached the age of 80 without wrinkles. But I don't find growing old so bad — it's very interesting and a challenge. And I'm still curious. I want to know everything all the time. I find the world infinitely amazing, beyond imagination and irresistible."

Marshall Perrow
putting the colour in water

Three years ago, architect-cum-artist Marshall Perrow was single-handing his Columbia 34 in Commencement Bay off Tacoma when he fell overboard. "I'd jibed," he recalls, "and the jib got fouled, so I went to the bow to free the sail. It went across with a bang. I tripped on the life line and over I went. The boat kept sailing."

Wisely, Marshall had worn his life jacket and, for security, had tied a 75-foot, knotted dockline to the boat's stern. He managed to swim over and grab the line. The boat continued at four knots and finally ran aground. "It was early June and very, very cold. I didn't think I was done for because I was too busy saving myself. When the boat hit bottom I pulled myself up to her hand over hand. After climbing back aboard — which took some doing — I confess I lay down for a while. Being immersed for half an hour had made me somewhat hypothermic." But he quickly stirred himself, got the jib down and back-winded the main to free the yacht. That's when he finally went below, changed his wet clothes and rested. After all, he was only 83.

His doctor, citing Marshall's "bit of heart trouble," told the octogenarian that his ticker would no longer tolerate this type of folly. "So," says Marshall, "I decided to try a powerboat." Never one to waste time, he sold his Columbia and bought a 43-foot Defever trawler, *Freedom*, which he's using summers as a floating studio for his sketching and photography. Winters, he retreats to the artist loft attached to the Tacoma home he's inhabited since he was 12 and transforms his sketches into watercolours. On the trawler, he shows me some of his originals, prints and posters, with their intense and cheerful colours. I particularly like his vibrant Caribbean harbour scenes and the depiction of the Tacoma tugboat races, capturing the tugs' muscle and daring.

Painting is not new to Marshall. It has complemented his career as an architect and his avocation as a boater. As a teenager, always handy with a tool, he built himself a 14-foot sailing dinghy. "I got the design out of *Popular Mechanics*. Took me two years. I was 16 when I finished it." While he was growing up, his well-off family owned a successful sporting goods store. But the Depression hit and money vanished, as did his father. To help support his mother and two younger brothers, Marshall attended school half-time and worked the other half. From junior high on, he knew he wanted to be an architect. "I was artistically inclined and drew all the time. I've made my own Christmas cards since I was a kid. Pen-and-ink drawings. And block prints from linoleum cuts. I would have liked to be an artist, but it was evident that I couldn't make any money at it. But architecture offered opportunities and I could still do the art."

Searching for work, the teenager applied at architectural offices, but in those wobbly financial times no one wanted to hire staff. "So I took a different tack and went to Gill, Mock and Morrison, the biggest firm in Tacoma. Told them I'd work for nothing all summer." Although taken aback, the firm gave him a try. After the second month, Marshall began earning 10 cents an hour. "That meant I could take the bus instead of walking to work." Senior partner Nelson Morrison, a talented artist and watercolourist, became Marshall's mentor and told the young man what classes to take in high school. Marshall is still grateful. "Nelson deeply influenced my career and I owe him a lot." By the time he graduated from high school, Marshall was a full-fledged draftsman earning a decent salary. As World War II loomed, he worked for wartime contractors and designed some large structures in Alaska. "There were about three big companies doing war jobs. I worked as a senior draftsman and junior designer for one of them as long as I was learning something; then I'd go to the next firm."

During his teenaged years, he also sailed and raced at the Tacoma Yacht Club and joined the Sea Scouts. Entering the navy reserves was the next logical step. During the war, now married to his high-school sweetheart, Marjorie, Marshall ended up as a chief warrant officer in the U.S. Coast Guard in Alaska, designing buildings and overseeing construction in coastal towns. He loved the architectural work, the skippering of 80-foot patrol boats and the fishing, hunting and sketching on his days off. "When my daughter Michelle asked me, 'Daddy, what did you do in the war that was heroic?' I told her that although I made my contribution, I didn't do a darn thing but have fun."

The war over, but still in uniform, Marshall sat for the Washington State architectural exams. "At that time, architectural school wasn't required. Having apprenticed was acceptable and many good architects went that route. I also joined the American Institute of Architects and am still a member."

He set up his own practice, but as he'd been away in the navy, he found jobs were scarce. Luck changed when a retired rear-admiral became a school-board trustee. "This guy noticed that all the architects who'd stayed home had big offices and commissions. He said, 'By god, the guys who were in the service ought to get a break.' So each of us servicemen got a school to design. Suddenly I had a big project and it led to my doing lots of schools."

Like so many people who grew up poor during the Depression, Marshall remained on the lookout for opportunities to provide lasting financial security. He bought an office building and besides schools, designed restaurants, homes, stores and shopping centres. He built the first ski tow in the west and started a ski school. He made industrial and promotional films. He maintained his architectural practice until two years ago. Even today, although financially comfortable, he still worries about money.

Marshall and Marjorie bought their first sailboat in 1943, a 31-foot Spencer. The purchase almost got him in trouble. He'd asked a buddy if he could use the ways at the Coast Guard yard to look at his new boat's bottom. "Then," he says, "some gosh darn do-gooder wrote a letter to the editor about the Coast Guard servicing sailing yachts in wartime. That sure ended my chances of keeping her at that yard!"

During the more than 50 years since World War II, he's never stopped painting or sailing. With improving finances, Marshall got himself both a new sailboat and a floatplane, which he flew to visit many of his design projects up and down the coast. It also served to bring him to the 33-foot Alden *Nixie*, which the family sailed in Puget Sound and the Inside Passage. During the summer, Marjorie and Michelle would stay on the vessel while Marshall travelled and occasionally rejoined them. They kept the Alden for 18 years, then replaced her with the Columbia 34, which Marshall calls a "Tupperware boat."

He's intensely proud of having "trained" his daughter for the boating life. Throughout the 1950s, when few people cruised in the Pacific Northwest, and fewer with children, they'd make the boat into their "cottage." "Michelle was quite gregarious. When we got to a new mooring or anchorage, she'd say, 'Well, I'm going to make some new friends,' and pretty soon there'd be two or three kids on the boat to see her doll or fishing tackle." Marshall also bought her a sailing dinghy when she was 11. One day, when the family was anchored at Tent Island near Saltspring, Michelle wanted to sail her dinghy. Despite being cautioned not to venture beyond the harbour's farthest point, she went on anyway and capsized. "Everybody said we should go help her. But I said no. So we watched her take down the sail in the water, right the boat, bail it, rehoist the sail and tack back, all without saying a word. Today, she's Washington State's ex-Deputy Secretary of State and running her own consulting business. I'm convinced she learned her self-reliance on those boats."

Marshall's floatplane also became a vehicle to satisfy his artistic yearnings. He flew up to the Queen Charlottes, sketching and drawing — and thus documenting — many of the now-deserted villages. Marshall sees these village abandonments as a great loss. "There are places on Anthony Island where the forests have encroached and overgrown the villages and longhouses.

The only authentic things left are the mortuary poles — unique, round, squat poles located outside the main village circulation — but they're just rotting away. I dug around in the blackberry bushes and found a few remains, beautiful wolf heads, and made paintings of them."

He'd seek out any Native art he could find, visiting carvers on Vancouver Island's west coast from whom he bought miniature dance masks. The artist he remembers most fondly lived in Haida Gwaii's Skidegate. "He was called Moses and carved argillite. You know, argillite is found in only two places: the Queen Charlottes and Mexico. When it's in the ground, it's quite soft, but once it's unearthed, the oxygen case-hardens it. I'd drop in on Moses, a huge guy working at a tiny little desk, and buy two or three of his carvings. He'd explain the history of each one. But he also showed me something funny. When he carved the argillite, it was greyish, but the finished products were black and shiny. I asked Moses how they got that way, thinking he used fish oil mixed with charcoal. He smiled, reached into his drawer and pulled out a can of Shinola shoe polish!"

A decade or so ago, Marshall found a non-architectural way to make his painting pay off: he became the resident artist on many cruise-ship voyages. The Holland America Line engaged him to teach watercolour painting when ships were at sea, with sometimes up to 40 people per class. He had ready sketches of ports of call from around the world. Malta, for example, with its old town and beautiful, overhanging balconies, made a great sample. He'd prepare a line drawing, copy it and the students would trace and expand it. Then he'd make a demonstration painting, showing the participants how to use colour. "At the end of two hours, they'd pretty well gotten a painting down. The little old ladies were so happy," he says, forgetting he's the same age as his students.

Marshall, accompanied by Marjorie, did more of those trips than he can remember, many in the Caribbean and Mediterranean. They enjoyed such places as Barcelona, Crete, Nice, Corsica, Genoa, Rome and Venice. They visited Turkey, Egypt and Israel. They passed through the Suez Canal, saw Aqaba and Petra, and ended up in Bombay, Malaysia and Singapore.

Three years ago, Marjorie died, leaving Marshall bereft and dejected. Only slowly did he start to re-engage himself in activities. He takes painting classes. "All my life I've been doing architectural renderings, which demands precision. I can do perspective. Now I'm trying to change my technique and get looser and more expressive." At one of the workshops, he met Californian Vera Reynolds, also widowed, and they travel together to art programs. She visits him on *Freedom* so she can sketch, and her occasional presence has perked him up. "We share an interest in painting," he says. "She's fun and, better yet, pays her own way."

He uses his trawler to find isolated or appealing sketching places. Last year, he shot photos and made sketches at the annual Whidbey Island regatta at Oak Harbor. "I also go ashore. I'm pretty mobile with a packsack, a carrying case with an easel and seat." He continues to produce an annual painting for the Coast Guard, used around the country as a recruitment tool. Three years ago, he won the Admiral's Award for "best painting," a scene depicting the wreck of a Coast Guard rescue ship. "It's the neatest specimen I ever did," he says proudly, nodding his head with its thick thatch of white hair.

The octogenarian remains frightfully busy. Over the next 10 years, he plans to catalogue his "tremendous backlog of paintings" and paint new ones. "I've got a one-man show coming up in Tacoma, and I've got to get another painting out to the Coast Guard to keep my official status." He's taking his boat to Hood Canal this summer, where his daughter and son-in-law attend a family camp, and Marshall has to teach a five-day watercolour workshop.

In the meantime, he's in a quandary about that darn powerboat. He can manoeuvre it all right, but jumping off quickly is a problem. "I am getting on a bit, you know." He's considering swapping the boat for a modest motor sailer. "A powerboat is dullsville; I'm just sitting at that wheel and grinding out the miles. We all know that, around here, you motor-sail 75 percent, but the sail is up and sometime you're going to use it. I'm just not ready to give it up. Because what I've learned in my 86 years is that the important thing is to have fun."

James Delgado
the shipwreck hunter

When readying himself to dive a shipwreck, Jim Delgado experiences excitement tinged with trepidation. How deep is it? How risky? Is his diving gear tiptop? Is the sunken ship so deteriorated it poses a danger? But once Jim enters the ocean's cocoon, where the water's buoyancy negates his bulky tanks and bodyweight, he sheds misgivings and grows calm. "My exhilaration builds as I drop," he says, "because I know I'll be touching the past. Not the past in a museum gallery, visible to everyone, but a past I may well be the first to see. It's magic." In the water, Jim explains, he has no sense of smell and is almost deaf. Here he achieves an extreme clarity of seeing, of developing the most focussed interaction with the remnants of history.

Surprisingly, Jim, the 44-year-old executive director of the Vancouver Maritime Museum and author of 24 books — most of them relating to underwater archeology, the history of ships and exploration by ship — grew up in semi-arid San Jose, California, about 60 miles south of San Francisco. Jim's interest in history and archeology was stirred in early childhood, but with an underground rather than an underwater focus. In his hometown, he often visited a local museum run by the Rosicrucians (who trace their origins back to ancient Egypt), where he saw his first mummy and crawled down into a mock-up tomb. He was transformed into an archeologist the night his father's cousin brought over a skeleton his bulldozer had scraped up while digging troughs. At that time, in the late 1960s, San Jose was on the cusp of metamorphosing into Silicon Valley. Housing developments, freeways and cloverleaves sprouted instantaneously, and one of the excavations for tract homes had disturbed a burial mound dating back 3,000 years. Besides hundreds of skeletons, the fields contained artifacts left by the Muwekma Ohlone tribes, which had inhabited the region for millennia, and items left by the later Spanish-Mexican colonizers, the Bernal family, who owned the Rancho de Santa Theresa.

The next day, after school, Jim biked to the building area. As there were no laws to protect historic sites, construction workers were taking skulls home as trophies. Jim argued with the foreman, then the developer, about preserving the graves. "I was brushed aside," says Jim, still outraged by the memory. "They said, 'What do you know, anyway? You're a kid standing in the way of progress. Who cares about old dead Indians and all this junk?'" Fortunately, a few archeologists from San Jose State University were doing salvage work, without authorization or funding, and they, taking note of the keen youngster, invited him into their midst. Thus began a long line of people who appreciated Jim and his inquisitive spirit. He worked with the archeologists throughout that year, learning, taking notes, recovering artifacts from bulldozer blades, cataloguing and cleaning. "My poor mother," says Jim. "She'd go into my room and find several skeletons in various stages of disarray. It drove her nuts."

One day, Jim borrowed a tie from his dad and asked San Jose mayor Norman Mineta (now U.S. Secretary of Transportation) to enact laws for the protection of historic sites. Mineta took him to the city's planners, who agreed that more should be done to safeguard the past. Jim was appointed to the city's Youth Commission and acted as liaison to the Landmark Commission — his first exposure to politics — a volunteer job he held throughout his teens, when he joined the Bicentennial Commission. He refined his view of history. "My interests weren't really with dead things, but with the past and making the past come to life. So I didn't try out for football or join the drama club. Instead, I found Bernal family descendants who lived all around San Jose and began writing up their history." He found another mentor, Greta Kleiner, and the pair drove around in an Austin Healey Sprite while they interviewed pioneers and explored crumbling adobe ruins. He also credits Lynn Vermillion, who managed the California History Room at the San Jose Public Library, with encouraging his zeal for history and introducing him to ideas and people. "These women had a strong impact on my life."

Jim's parents supported him guardedly in his explorations. For Christmas, he'd receive dental picks, trowels and archeology books; they'd drop him off at the Egyptian Museum where he volunteered; and, one summer, they allowed him to participate in a dig 200 miles away. But they worried about his obsessions. "Their biggest fear was that my interests would never develop into a career," he explains. "My dad was the son of Mexican immigrants and had lifted himself up by the bootstraps by becoming a fireman. My mom was a homemaker." When Jim decided he wanted to attend the local university, his parents, suggesting he could transfer to a university later, encouraged him to attend the community college instead. It didn't have a history program, however. Downhearted, Jim confided in Lynn Vermillion, his librarian friend. She called the chair of the San Jose State history department and he visited Jim's parents in their home. "When I walked into the kitchen that night, my parents told me I was going to San Jose State as a history major. I don't have to tell you I was thrilled."

Jim learned a valuable lesson that day. "In life," he says with some emotion in his voice, "you get by through the kindness of friends and strangers and with their tolerance and support. I also know that you have to work for what you get; you must pay your dues. So off I went to the university, lived at home and graded papers to make money." Two years later, he was hired as an assistant to the regional historian for the National Park Service in San Francisco. For Jim, this was another sea change. Construction of the Transamerica Pyramid had hit a buried ship, the *Niantic*, a Connecticut whaler, abandoned by its crew in 1849 and hauled ashore to serve as a storeship. She burned to the mud line in 1851 and her hulk was jettisoned. "I was spellbound watching the wreck emerge from the ground," Jim recalls. "Buried in mud and 24 feet beneath the street. As they lifted the stern, the hull's copper sheath was as bright as a new penny and the rudder still swung on its hinges." Jim was assigned the task of inventorying the goods remaining in the hull, reporting on the *Niantic*'s fate and nominating it to the National Register of Historic Places. And Jim, eyeing the burnt hulk still clutching its tins of pâté, bottles of champagne, brass paper clamps, pencils from London and only partially eroded guns, fell in love with another aspect of history and archeology: ships.

For the next few years, Jim's life resembled a rollercoaster ride. Someone once described him as a "young man in a hurry," and he seemed intent on fulfilling that portrayal. He finished his history degree magna cum laude at San Francisco State while working full-time as a ranger, interpreter and then park historian at the Golden Gate National Recreational Area with its 2,000 buildings, the Presidio, the Maritime Museum and over a hundred shipwrecks. He learned about sail handling on old schooners; he married and became father to a son, John. "I was just an activist," Jim says enthusiastically, "and tromped around, surveyed, added things to the National Register and crawled through the tunnels of Alcatraz. We even dug up a temporary Civil War gun battery that had been built to defend San Francisco from Confederate raiders." The army unit stationed at the Presidio taught him how to dive, and with the park archeologist, Marty Mayer, he started working on a wrecked gold-rush steamship, the *Tennessee*.

In the mid 1980s, the Park Service gave Jim a furlough and he and his family — now including a baby daughter, Darcy — moved to North Carolina so he could earn a master's degree in underwater archeology at East Carolina University. While writing his thesis on the shipwrecks of the Cape Hatteras National Seashore, he was once again at the right place for a shift in government interests. Ed Bearss, the National Park Service's chief historian for military sites, invited Jim to serve as project historian on a plan of the Park Service and the National Oceanic & Atmospheric Administration to study and preserve the wreck of the USS *Monitor*. This U.S. Civil War ship was the world's first ironclad, turreted warship and fought an inconclusive battle with another, larger, ironclad, the CSS *Virginia*, in March 1862. On New Year's Eve that same year, the *Monitor* sank in a fierce storm 16 miles south of Cape Hatteras in 230 feet of water. Although the ship foundered, her existence portended the end of wooden battleships. Jim wrote the historic National Landmark study for the *Monitor*, and this project led to the next: an inventory and ranking of marine resources in the U.S. Jim had a friend in the computer business who showed him how to catalogue the preserved ships, shipwrecks, museums and lighthouses in a sortable database instead of on the traditional index-card system.

At the age of 29, Jim was hired to head the new federal Maritime Preservation Program and serve as Maritime Historian for the Park Service, jobs that required the family to relocate to Washington, D.C. Over the next four years, Jim, believing he needed to be "hands on," spent more than half his time on the road: diving in Pearl Harbor and Bikini Atoll; negotiating treaties and agreements on lost ships with the Mexicans, British, French and Canadians; inventorying more than 300 ships; going out on active navy ships; photographing and archiving; designating ships for the National Register — a whirlwind of activity. Office duties, budget preparation and the politics of federal service also made their demands. He paid a price. His intensity didn't always make him popular and the stress of moving across the country, his constant travel, and his son being diagnosed with severe autism and needing special care led to the break-up of his marriage. Yet looking back at it, Jim sees this professional period as seminal. "I think it was the most incredible educational experience I ever had. Some sort of portal into maritime history. I dived over 100 shipwrecks, visited every maritime museum. I passionately believed in the mission and had lots of fun. There's something about seeing all of it first-hand and touching it."

One day in 1990, a Vancouver head-hunter called Jim asking for the names of people who might qualify as director of the Vancouver Maritime Museum. Maybe Jim was tired of advising others how to preserve their maritime history and then moving on to the next project; perhaps new federal regulations prohibiting civil servants from lecturing or writing publicly in their areas of expertise thwarted his ambitions; possibly his breakneck travel schedule had lost its allure. He sent in his own résumé, was hired and moved back to the Pacific, this time in a different country. Moving to Canada was more of a shock than he'd anticipated. Taxes were high and milk, cheese and gasoline cost more. And then there was his personal style. "In Washington, everything was go-for-the-throat aggressive and I was in that mindset when I moved here. Once I had that sorted out, there was an awful lot I liked about Canada. I liked the fact you didn't have to win by conquering people. That you could reach consensus. And the pace of life is good. That said, I still work very hard."

When Jim arrived, the museum was in disarray. "I really hunkered down the first years," Jim says. "The place was horribly in debt, staff had left, the board was dissatisfied, the infrastructure was crumbling." *St. Roch* (the historic RCMP ship that served in the Canadian Arctic for decades and is the museum's centrepiece) was managed by Parks Canada, and its staff was at odds with that of the museum. Jim brought to bear his experience in the U.S. Park Service, and counting on the fact he "spoke parks language," began mending fences. "Things were tough and I was hanging on by my fingertips," he says. "No writing or extracurricular activities except for a small guidebook on *St. Roch*, for which there was no literature." By 1997, Jim, working with a strong board of directors and a more supportive community, had increased museum attendance, wiped out the deficit and planned new projects. He supported the RCMP re-enactment of *St. Roch's* circumnavigation of North America, a fund-raising voyage with the intent of restoring the old vessel crumbling inside its A-frame. He organized an Arctic field project on Roald Amundsen's ship, the *Maud*. The research resulted in Jim's writing *Across the Top of the World*, which sold over 50,000 copies. "I loved doing it and it's one of my favourite books," Jim says with gusto. "It also marked a big change for me. Working at the museum, doing exhibits and seeing how people respond brought me back to my time as a ranger. What I really want to be is not an archeologist, historian or museum person, but a storyteller, using the past to inspire and excite people, making it accessible for everyone. *Across the Top of the World* was written with that in mind, a popular book based on informed scholarship, with clear, readable text, humour and lots of photos and reproductions of paintings. One reviewer got the point and said, 'It's a coffee-table book with a brain.'"

Now back in the writing vein, Jim has written three children's books on underwater archeology and penned the centennial history of the Royal Vancouver Yacht Club, a tome called *Never Luff, Never Reef*, with the proceeds going to the Vancouver Maritime Museum. As is his wont, he continues to move beyond hull speed. He's completing his doctoral dissertation at Simon Fraser University, a compendium of all the 75 ships buried in San Francisco, and looks forward to hosting his parents in Vancouver when he becomes "Dr." Delgado. He's contemplating an autobiographical "Confessions of a Sea Hunter" to take people along on a tour of the great shipwrecks. He'd like to include a vessel that foundered in 1281 off southern Japan and the wrecks he's dived on Clive Cussler's television show "Sea Hunter," which include the *Titanic*, the *Carpathia*, the *Mary Celeste* and the minesweeper HMCS *Clayoquot*, sunk off Halifax on Christmas Eve, 1944.

Jim has married Ann Goodhart, chief librarian at the West Vancouver Library. He's happy. "I like the fact," he says, "that in a job like this you can be a storyteller and give people an opportunity to connect with the past. I am a lucky guy. I write, lecture, curate, dive, dig and host a television show. But all of it is tied together with that thread that started so long ago: touching the past and having the past come to life. Not just looking at the thing but looking at the people behind the thing — the story of real people — because that's the meaning of history."

Margo Wood
Charlie's choice

When Margo Wood was about to be born, her father inexplicably hitched up the sleigh and drove away from their northern Alberta homestead to visit a neighbour. Fortunately, Margo's mother, a self-reliant nurse, was able to deliver the baby unassisted. No doubt her mother's strength, combined with the struggle to survive the lean Depression years, contributed to Margo's grit. She earned a university degree (unlikely for her gender and the times), defied her parents by marrying Charles Wood and then cruised with him without knowing how to sail — or swim. Their explorations led to *Charlie's Charts*, some of the earliest and most popular cruising guides in the Pacific region, which Margo continues to write, update, publish and distribute today. Her recent autobiography, *A Prairie Chicken Goes to Sea*, details her childhood, her life with Charles and how she learned to survive on a boat, growing confident enough that, eventually, she sailed solo.

Margo, born in Alberta's Peace River country in 1934, now lives in White Rock, B.C., just north of the U.S. border. She has a big welcoming smile and a cap of snow-white hair that frames her youngish face. The day I meet her, she's matched her sky-blue jumpsuit to her eyes. In between Alberta and White Rock, she's travelled to many places, her wanderlust stimulated by an unlikely source: Blue Ribbon Tea. In the 1940s, each box of tea her mother bought was accompanied by an envelope of cancelled foreign stamps, which Margo collected and glued into a notebook, and the colourful bits of paper from those exotic countries seized her imagination. Scrutinizing them in the family's unpainted, isolated farmhouse, she daydreamed that one day, she'd see the world. When she graduated from university, she began planning, figuring she'd teach business education for two years, save her money and make a trip around the world. Then she met Charles Wood, a mountaineer and outdoor enthusiast who'd already travelled on a budget in Europe. They fell in love and planned to wed, but Margo's parents strenuously opposed her marriage because they considered Charles, born in Burma, "of indeterminate racial background." Although her parents refused to meet Charles, Margo married him in 1958 and the newlyweds spent six months backpacking and camping in Europe. Upon their return, they settled in Vancouver where Margo again taught business education and Charles enrolled at the University of British Columbia to study engineering.

It was Charles who dreamed of owning a sailboat; Margo was lukewarm. For her, sailing evoked visions of shipwrecks and drowned sailors. Moreover, she didn't swim. But Charles was persuasive and Margo wanted to prove she was a good sport. Their first boat was the yawl *Delos*, and their inexperience led them to ignore such dangers as a cockpit that drained into the bilge. She was a heavy vessel, with poor sails and untuned rigging. Charles claimed he knew how to sail, but Margo wrote later, "[He was] bluffing, talking a good line, but it was entirely based on theory! I was oblivious to the fact we were the only vessel in the water with a captain and crew who had to refer to a book merely to sail out of the bay."

Very slowly, the reluctant first mate learned sailing terminology and lost at least part of her fear of water. *Delos*, however, was riddled with dry rot and the pair was forced to sell her as a do-it-yourself special. Undeterred, they purchased a 36-foot centre-board Crocker ketch they named *Kakoodlak*, the Inuit word for "bird of the storm." They lived aboard, an unconventional lifestyle at the time, and after gaining more experience in coastal cruising, they began planning a four-to-five-year circumnavigation. Full of anticipation, they set off from Vancouver in August

1963. A gale followed by a storm off the Washington and Oregon coasts made Charles so violently seasick that he was greatly weakened. His fragility, coupled with a broken steering quadrant, led to their being towed into San Francisco by the Coast Guard. Demoralized, they put the boat up for sale, returned to Vancouver, bought a house and became "normal" people. For a while, at least.

When Charles was offered a two-year position in Toronto, the couple again caught the sailing bug. They found a sturdy, 34-foot mahogany cutter built by Nova Scotia's John Barkhouse and christened her *Ern*, after the European sea eagle. After Charles had completed his work assignment, the pair collected the boat in Sarnia, crossed Lake Erie and traversed the Erie Barge Canal with its more than 40 locks, then joined the Hudson River at Albany, New York. They continued on through New York City, navigated the Intracoastal Waterway and spent a warm-water winter in the Bahamas. When their savings ran low, they shipped *Ern* back to Vancouver and once again returned to a conventional lifestyle. They adopted a baby boy, Devereau, and were looking to give him a sister when Margo was diagnosed with cervical cancer. Fortunately, her surgery was successful and after her recovery, daughter Charmian joined the family. Margo, realizing she couldn't save a child who might fall overboard, finally learned to swim. She also joined a women's sailing group and thus, she recalls, "For the first time in my sailing life I was no longer limited to the cockpit following the captain's instructions." Another change occurred when Margo's parents, abandoning their fears of miscegenation once the children were adopted, renounced their nine-year silence and made "a reconciliation of sorts."

Once again, the sea nudged the Woods. Now that the family had expanded, they decided on a larger boat, so they sold *Ern* and acquired a Spencer 51 hull, with the intention of completing the interior themselves. Then Charles suddenly had a serious heart attack, one that not only diminished the 46-year-old's physical vigour for good, but also made him irritable and self-centred. Margo struggled with the change in her husband's personality, and as

Charles's engineering work diminished, she went back to teaching once again to pay for the family's bills and the finishing of the boat. Charles recovered slowly, and once more they began planning an offshore cruise. After *Frodo* was launched in 1975, the family decided on a coast-hopping voyage to minimize stress on Charles's heart. Stopping frequently to avoid overnight passages, they made it to Mexico, where they anchored in bays and inlets recommended by other yachties. Charles made sketches of these anchorages and, encouraged by boaters they met along the way, sent his drawings and text to *Cruising World*, which promptly published them. He also wrote a book, *Building Your Dream Boat*, and a series of technical articles for *Sail* and *Cruising World*. Nevertheless, it became clear that sailing to weather was too strenuous for Charles, and reluctantly they sold *Frodo* and returned to work and school in Vancouver. One day, as Charles glanced at the newspaper's "boats for sale" section, he saw *Ern* was back on the market. Thus the mahogany cutter re-entered their lives; Margo still owns her today.

Over the next years, sailors frequently sent letters asking for more of Charles's hand-drawn renderings of Mexican anchorages, so when Harry Merrick, who published a Mexican guide called *Baja Traveler*, offered Charles aerial trips to survey the Mexican coast, he eagerly accepted. He produced not only photographic bird's-eye views of anchorages, but a hand-drawn set of sea profiles and critical harbour entrances. Merrick was interested only in the photos, and thus the drawings became the basis for creating *Charlie's Charts of the Western Coast of Mexico*, although Charles, a formal fellow, winced at the familiar adaptation of his name. Because the *Dream Boat* book hadn't produced much in the way of royalties, Margo and Charles opted to self-publish the guide — quite uncommon in the early 1980s. In 1981, they printed 1,000 copies; the edition sold out in a year.

Encouraged, Charles flew to French Polynesia, where he sailed with friends and chartered boats to produce a guide on those islands' ports and anchorages. A sail to Hawaii, followed by several more trips by plane, resulted in a Hawaiian Islands guide. Meanwhile, Margo taught school, ran the household, raised the kids and acted as business manager for *Charlie's Charts*. Wanting to be out on the boat herself, she suggested a cruising guide to Alaska. With a friend, Charles went up in *Em* and Margo joined them for the voyage south from Sitka. A year later, *Charlie's Charts North to Alaska* joined the roster. The couple realized cruisers now had guides from the U.S. border north to Alaska and from the U.S. border south to Mexico: a guide to the Pacific coast from Seattle to San Diego would fill the gap. This time, they drove down the coast, which they had visited by boat in the past, with Charles sketching the harbours, and Margo collecting information on marine and other supplies, fuel sources and grocery stores.

After their return at summer's end in 1987, Margo received a phone call at school. Working too hard on a government contract he'd obtained for his engineering firm, Charles had suffered another heart attack. He died a few days later, at the age of 59.

Margo felt both sad and angry to be widowed at the age of 53. When she tried to teach her high-school courses, grief overwhelmed her. She took a leave of absence and, almost on autopilot, continued filling orders for *Charlie's Charts*. The U.S. Pacific Coast guide with Charles's hand-drawn charts languished on a shelf. Then one day, Margo grew determined to complete this portion of Charles's legacy. She resigned her teaching job and, needing someone to write the guide's text, called John Guzzwell, author of *Trekka Round the World*, asking for his help. John, however, was building a boat and suggested she compose the text herself. Although insecure about her writing abilities, she began drafting the copy, writing and rewriting, polishing and honing. When she finished the guide, her name appeared on the cover below Charles's, unlike the earlier ones. "A friend once told me Charles was a Victorian man," explains Margo. "She was right. Charles had the view 'what I say goes,' and women, well, he didn't like to accept me as a full partner. Even though I was equally involved in putting the guides together, there wasn't any question he'd be the only author."

Figuring that without Charles, Margo would be unable to sustain *Charlie's Charts*, some opportunists tried to latch on to the cruising guides' success. A retired hydrographer with an impressive résumé approached her and offered to prepare a guide for Fiji and Tonga. Margo was intrigued. "'Wow, this fellow knows what he's doing,' I said to myself, so I asked for a proposal. The response was a two-page, single-spaced list itemizing the expenses to be charged against the guide's production. He'd included a daily rate of $100 for his boat, another $100 for his work, $50 for his wife, $50 for the dinghy and outboard, plus some smaller extra outlays. These daily costs would be incurred for one summer, and he'd charge the same rate again when I flew down to do fact-checking. When I tallied up the costs for putting the book together, plus travel and printing, I'd have had to sell each guide for $200 to break even. Obviously, he priced himself out of the market."

Margo continued to develop her sea legs. In 1991, she wrote a cruising guide on her own. "That was a hoot," she recalls with a chuckle. "Some of the San Diego dealers told me that so many cruisers were going to Costa Rica I should give it a go. 'Well,' I thought, 'it's a small country and it's only the west coast.'" She flew down with Maurice Brager, a widower who's become her "best buddy," rented a small pickup truck and charted the coast from the shore and from chartered boats. It doesn't contain Charles's "outstanding sea views" as Margo puts it, but she's proud of having completed a guide under her own name. Meanwhile, she regularly updates the other five, travelling the coasts, receiving letters and e-mails with corrections and new items from yachties who consider the guides their "bible." Certain delivery skippers also keep Margo informed of such changes as reconfigured docks, a new restaurant or a change in fuelling opportunities. For each new edition — the guide to Mexico is now in its 21st — Margo visits every harbour herself to ensure all data is current. The guides to the U.S. Pacific Coast and to Mexico sell more than 1,000 copies a year; the others sell about half that number.

As a multitude of small production vessels has made boating less costly and thus more popular, cruising-guide competition has grown as well. Today, cruising-guide authors elbow each other at boat shows. "The rivalry is basically friendly enough," says Margo, "but once *Charlie's Charts* were the only show in town. Now there are so many I've had to get out of my little shell to do more seminars and wave the flag at boat shows in Seattle and Vancouver."

Margo's ardour for travel has never waned. With *Em*, she practised docking and anchoring on her own. She took a course in diesel mechanics, then in electrical systems and electronic navigation. Although fearful at first, she single-handed. In 2000, she signed up as a steward on the *Simon Fraser*, the Coast Guard icebreaker that accompanied *St. Roch II* on its historic re-enactment in the Arctic. She thought the voyage, whose first leg travelled from Halifax to Vancouver through the Panama Canal before the ship went on to transit the Arctic with *St. Roch II*, would be "a neat adventure," and she loved the safety and firefighting training she took to qualify. Unfortunately, the voyage turned out to be painful and unhappy, with the crew divided into warring camps. Margo and Doreen, another volunteer, were singled out for harassment by the assistant cook. "She decided we didn't fit in," says Margo. "We were considered the 'ladies,' because we didn't swear, smoke or tie one on every other night. The captain had a Bligh-like personality. By the time we got to Vancouver, more than half the crew skedaddled because the atmosphere was poison."

But that bad experience doesn't deter her from going out on the water. In fact, accompanied by Frank Eberlein, a young oiler she met on the icebreaker, she sailed *Em* to the Queen Charlottes and around Vancouver Island in 2001. She's waiting to have the cartilage in her knee repaired ("I can't take the twisting motion on the boat") so she can continue sailing. "I want to keep on doing what I've been doing," she says fervently. "There are all kinds of places on the coast that I haven't seen. And I'm sure there are going to be more *Charlie's Charts*. I love the travel and meeting other yachtsmen, the involvement and the action."

Margo has a definite message for women and boats. She recommends gaining as much knowledge as possible from every source — books and courses. "Once you've got some confidence in yourself, go for it, don't hold back," she says. "Naval

Commander Ted Walker once said, 'Grab a chance and you won't be sorry for a might-have-been.' That's why I'm glad Charles and I had those adventures and I have all these memories." But she also has advice for husbands who want their wives to enjoy the boating life. After Charles died, she read some of his logs. "He wasn't always as pleasant as he could have been, but in the log he complimented me a number of times. But never verbally. Why couldn't he have said, 'Good show, Margo, that was great'? So in my seminars and in my book, I tell men to communicate with their partners. To encourage them. To become a team."

Margo sees herself as the guardian of Charles's legacy. "He gave me and countless others confidence to cruise up and down these coasts," she says with some pride. "I wouldn't have gone to sea alone. His drive made it possible and I'm still benefitting. Although I'll never circumnavigate the world, I can still go off to an anchorage and absorb nature, the scenery, peace and tranquillity. Elbert Hubbard wrote at the beginning of the last century, 'The greatest mistake a man can make is to be afraid of making one.' That's what epitomizes my life."

Tom Kincaid
the boating publisher

It was the unemployment line in Port Angeles, Washington, that serendipitously turned Tom Kincaid into a magazine publisher. Having struck out on tuna fishing, Tom was looking for a job. While he was completing some application forms, the manager wandered by and peeked over Tom's shoulder. "So you've been in the oyster business, huh?" he asked Tom. After Tom's affirmative answer, the manager said, "Well, I'm the program chair for our local Lions Club. How would you like to give a talk on oyster growing? Our next meeting is in about an hour."

"That was the start of my public-speaking career," Tom grins. "And a sea change in my life." Charles Webster, publisher of the *Port Angeles Evening News*, was in the Lions Club audience, liked what he heard and eventually offered Tom a job as an ad salesman. Although he had no advertising experience, Tom took to the life, and while selling ads up and down the Olympic Peninsula, he discovered stories that needed to be written. Thus the man whose earlier career track had focussed exclusively on salty trades became a features writer. About a decade later, in 1965, he co-founded *Nor'westing*, the first magazine devoted entirely to Pacific Northwest boating.

Before Tom was ready for this risky entrepreneurial undertaking, he'd had a long apprenticeship on the water. When he speaks about his long life (he was born in 1923), it's clear that he's actively participated in most of the 20th century's national and regional events: youth during the Depression, military service during World War II, the boom and bust of the logging and fishing industries, revolutions in environmental standards, the explosive growth of recreational boating. Family life exposed him to boating from the time he was in swaddling clothes. His father was a University of Washington marine biology professor who started a biological research station in Friday Harbor. Thus, in his early years, Tom and his siblings often visited San Juan Island, where they roamed around in rowboats and on the university's research vessels. By the time he reached his teens, Tom yearned for his own boat.

He teamed up with a high-school buddy with whom he'd raced Flatties. "We both had paper routes and had about two nickels in our jeans, but not much more," he recalls. "We knew we'd have to buy lumber and parts so we saved our money and started looking at plans." To locate drawings, the fledgling boat-building team searched the public library. There, they chanced upon a little book, *Twenty-one Boats and How to Build Them*, by Ed Monk, which included plans for the perfect 21-footer. The duo began gathering "wood and screws and stuff" and laid out the transom and stem in the living room of Tom's friend's house. They outgrew that space when they started building the frames and began scouting for a larger site. They managed to rent a section in an abandoned sawmill on Portage Bay's north shore for $5 a month, but the owner, who liked the boys' gumption, never collected the rent. Just the opposite. He often ambled by and lent the young men tools they couldn't afford. The boat-building team's ambition grew and they resolved to add a cuddy cabin to their open boat, a change requiring design adaptations. "With our alterations, we worried about the balance of the mainsail versus the jib. Were we getting ourselves in trouble? So I made a sketch of our proposed cabin, caught the streetcar and went to Ed Monk's office. After I knocked, a tall slender gentleman in a brown suit with a perfect tie and shiny shoes opened the door. He looked down at me and said, 'What can I do for you?' Then he spent the next three hours carefully teaching me what I needed to know to do the job right." Aided by Ed Monk's instructions, the young men finished their carvel-planked boat.

Tom's father's expertise in marine biology led to his involvement with the Japanese oyster (*Crassostrea gigas*) business then starting on the west coast. He acquired some oyster beds at Willapa Harbor on the Columbia River near Astoria, where Tom began working in the summers from the age of 15 on. He ran boats and towed barges, and when the seasonal oyster farming reached "a dead spot," he went gillnetting for salmon. After high school, he had a chance to lease an oyster-opening operation. He liked running his own business, shucking oysters and selling them to markets in Portland and other cities, but World War II interfered with enterprise and, in 1942, he entered the air force. Although ready to go overseas, he remained stateside for the duration. "They made a celestial navigation instructor out of me, even though all I'd ever done was eyeball dead-reckoning. They sent me to school and I then taught air force navigators. I liked it better in hindsight than I did at the time. But I got to fly whenever I wanted, although flying in a bomber isn't like crossing the country in a passenger plane. We had some adventures flying over Minnesota in the wintertime in front of an open window at 180 knots ... "

While stationed at Illinois's Chinoot Field, he met Louise and married her, and by the end of the war, the couple returned to Seattle with their first child. Tom went back to university to study chemical engineering, but found it hard "to get back into an academic frame of mind." He decided to return to oyster farming, but opted to cultivate the indigenous Olympia oysters instead of the beefy Japanese imports. That profession gave him fundamental lessons in both resource depletion and in pollution. Once, he tells me, these tiny oysters grew in fat layers on rocky shores from Southern California to Alaska. San Francisco had grown large enough to have developed a vigorous appetite for oysters. "The Indians did the hard work and loaded the oysters onto sailing ships. Essentially, these businesses stripped oysters out of the bays close to San Francisco and gradually worked their way up the coast. Nobody thought of conservation in those days. The only little oysters left were in the small corner bays down in the south end of Puget Sound. In those narrow passages with contrary winds, it was too damn hard to get a sailboat in."

In one far southwest cove off Puget Sound, near Shelton, Olympia oysters still thrived. A Japanese family had bought land there, ensured there was plenty of cultch for new sets, harvested oysters selectively and built a sustainable business. "But," Tom continues his historical account, "Pearl Harbor was bombed and the Japanese were interned. By the time they got their grounds back, the Shelton pulp mill had been discharging its pulp liquor full of sulphuric acid into the bay and killed off all the oysters. The Japanese sued (my father testified on their behalf) and the pulp company settled with them. Then the pulp mill piped their effluent into a valley behind Shelton. Gradually the bay cleaned up and the Japanese started raising oysters again, but five years later, they died once more. The pulp waste had soaked the ground and leached into a creek emptying into the bay. Another suit. Another settlement. This time the pulp mill ran its pipe about 10 miles out the inlet and stuffed their waste in tanks until the ebb tide could carry it out of Puget Sound. The Japanese moved." In the late 1940s, Tom, believing that oysters could again be successfully cultivated in this area, leased the land. For a year, he and Louise tried everything — growing and shucking oysters, digging clams — but they barely scraped by. "The demand was there," says Tom, "but I couldn't raise enough oysters to make a living."

Scouting for other opportunities to support his growing family, Tom bumped into a man towing a clutch of logs behind his tug. Called a "log patrolman," he was a state-licensed salvager cruising the shorelines and waters to collect branded logs which had popped loose from booms. Tom learned that a licensed buyer paid salvagers for recovered logs, which would then be returned to the owner. The patrolman told Tom he could make $300 to $400 on a good day. Tom, who considered a monthly income of $500 a good living, talked it over with Louise, and the family moved to Port Angeles, where no salvager had yet obtained a licence. Tom used his 22-foot runabout to collect logs on Juan de Fuca Strait. He liked the freedom of being on the water, and although he wasn't getting rich, he was able to support the family. Tom met a young boat builder who was finishing a 48-foot troller and the two formed a log-patrolling partnership, with Tom scouting the beaches in his small boat and the troller serving as tow boat. Then they got the idea of buying a surplus amphibious assault vessel. Tom guffaws when he recalls the challenge of running this ungainly hybrid. "It was a truck driven by a propeller in the water and by wheels on land. They'd been used for amphibious attacks throughout the Pacific war. Although they had huge Jimmy engines, they made only three knots max and had huge pumps because the trucks' low freeboard meant they were always filling up with water. We theorized we could drive up on a beach, winch a log with the steel cable and just drive back in the water. It worked fine, but we had to learn some 'boat-truck' techniques, like making sure the prop was up and the wheels down at the right second."

The partners also tried tuna fishing, but prices fell too low to sustain them, so they sold their boats and Tom took a job as boatman for the Puget Sound Pilots. That's when he gave his fateful Lions Club talk, which led to the newspaper ad sales job and his (unpaid) feature writing. "They liked the fact I was bringing in both revenue and stories," he says without any sense of irony. So much so that when the paper's editor, Earl Clark, bought a weekly newspaper, the *Edmonds Tribune Review*, he invited Tom along. The family moved again and Tom worked for the *Trib* until it was sold, then took over as publisher of another "old-fashioned weekly newspaper."

Throughout this period, Tom sailed with his family on a 30-foot, double-planked Herreshoff. The idea of starting a boating magazine had been bubbling in the back of his mind. In 1965, when his friend Ole Hansen returned from a sail to the South Pacific, Tom decided the time was right for this enterprise. "Ole had made a good living as a salesman and knew how to talk to people. I figured he'd be manager, I'd be editor. We created a dummy issue with a bunch of stories and pictures and went around to potential advertisers in the greater Seattle area." The partners received a positive response and *Nor'westing* was born. At first they borrowed time on the printing presses of the local newspaper, but eventually they bought their own linotype machine, which Tom calls the "Rube Goldberg computer" of the day. He recalls those halcyon days with joy. "As a magazine, we had no competition. *Sea* had started in Seattle but moved to California, so we had the market to ourselves." He remembers running the magazine with Ole as the most enjoyable way of making a living anybody's ever had. "I don't remember us having any problems working together," he says with enthusiasm. "I'm sure Ole and I disagreed on how to approach things from time to time, but this was our way of getting ideas on the table and deciding which was the best way. We never spoke a cross word to each other in 35 years."

Tom and Ole bought a powerboat to cover boating events and also used it for their monthly cruising story. After working frantically at production time ("We wanted to keep the ads as current as possible, so we put the magazine together at the last second"), they'd put the boat in gear. Wherever they ended up became the following month's destination tale. Their second "corporate yacht" was a 48-foot Norwegian troller. Tom took a bunk out of the former fish hold and installed a desk. "I did all my writing on that boat. What a great place to work. The magazine gave us a good living, not because we paid ourselves a lot, but when you own a boating magazine, it cuts the cost of living a bit. We depreciated the boat every year, never left the dock unless it was for business purposes, and paid for insurance and moorage through the business. In that way, we could have the use of a pretty big yacht without making lots of money."

Tom eventually sold the magazine but still contributes a monthly column. He's built a 10-foot wooden skiff in his workshop and when he needs a break, he sails his tiny cockleshell. "I've sailed for seven decades and still learn something every time I go out. When I'm on salt water I'm never far from the thought that this is where life started. That this water passing by my bow washed past Japan and Australia and Norway and Russia. That it joins the whole world. Yet I'm free to go anywhere I want on it. We humans are pretty much stuck to two dimensions and most of our lives are restricted by the yellow line. In a boat you don't have any yellow lines. Although you must follow some rules, there's a sense of freedom that's very refreshing. If I want to tack, I can, and there's no cop telling me I shouldn't. Sailing comes as close as you can get to flying, and I do mean sailing as opposed to powerboating. We used our powerboat as a tool in our business, but sailing is what I do for enjoyment. The idea of coaxing forward motion out of a breeze because of the shape of a hull and the sails is the most satisfying thing in the world."

Joan Austen-Leigh
the doppelganger

Joan Austen-Leigh. Joan Mason Hurley. Two names. One woman. A woman who charted a course between the literary legacy and sensibilities of her great-great-great aunt, Jane Austen, and her modern life as a bestselling novelist, award-winning playwright, wife, mother of four, hotel keeper and solo yachtswoman. Joan was born an Austen-Leigh, daughter of a British immigrant land surveyor and the bride he brought back to B.C. after the Great War. Her second double-barrelled name was acquired when she married Denis Mason Hurley in 1940.

The plural names reflected the two sides of her personality: as Mason Hurley, she wrote intrepid, humorous tales about plying the local waters in the *Elizabeth Bennet* with its tender *Mr. Darcy*. Under that moniker, she also penned more than 30 energetic, feisty plays, some with a decidedly feminist slant. Under the Austen-Leigh banner, she published two novels based on characters from *Emma*, written in 18th-century epistolary style, and also *Stephanie* and *Stephanie at War*, coming-of-age fiction that confirms her pride in her Canadian roots.

The twinning effect was even heard in Joan's voice — although she was born and bred in Victoria, her British-born parents and their friends ensured that her accent would fit nicely in a *Pride and Prejudice* Longbourn drawing room. In fact, if we can imagine Jane Austen leaving those same parlours, swapping her Empire-style gowns for foulies to sail B.C.'s straits and bays, she and her great-great-great niece would have a jolly time and hardly notice the 145-year age gap.

For her last 20-plus years, Joan sailed her 29-foot Bayfield cutter through the Gulf and San Juan islands, often single-handedly. Hers were not the daredevil tactics of a racer. "I'm a fair-weather sailor," she says with her precise diction. "I never went great distances. It was not the goal to go far. The goal was to be on my boat, on the water."

Joan was the daughter of thoroughly British parents who viewed this provincial capital on the edge of the North American continent as yet another outpost of the empire on which the sun never set. The wives who could afford it had servants, hosted parties and played bridge. Girls were raised to find a good husband and marry early. To fit in properly, to be "finished," Joan was sent to boarding school back "home" in the East Anglia town of Aldeburgh. Joan likens her experience there to "incarceration," but it did allow her to first step onto a sailboat on the River Alde at the age of 16.

Her first *real* sailing experience, however, occurred on Vancouver Island's Shawnigan Lake in a 19-foot, centreboard Flattie. "After showing me the ropes, my husband, Denis, pushed me offshore," she recalls. "I was on my own and had to do it alone. I learned I liked being in charge of the boat. Boats have added such a dimension to my life. Let me see things I'd never have seen and meet people I'd never have known. I can't imagine life without sailing."

She adds that while raising her brood, she had less time for this avocation, especially during the quarter century she and Denis managed the Shawnigan Beach Hotel. From May to October during this era, family-run hotels like theirs booked people by the week, which included all meals and such entertainment as dancing, horse racing, fishing, swimming and canoeing ($125 a week for two).

Still, although their lives were hectic, boats remained part of life on the lake. Joan's daughter Freydis remembers open wooden boats from 16 to 20 feet long with names like *Forest Nymph*, *Titwillow* and *Forest Sprite*. "The most extraordinary vessel we ever owned was made of Styrofoam," Joan says. "That boat had red-and-white striped sails, measured about 14 feet overall and we bought it for $105 at the Hudson's Bay Company. It had an aluminum mast and a wooden centreboard and tiller. My husband was most distressed because I took it out on Cadboro Bay on a very windy day."

A more "proper" Columbia 21 followed the Styrofoam vessel. "We'd moved to Victoria by then," Joan explains, "and after all those years of dinghy sailing, I had a boat with a cabin, a piece of shag carpet, a berth and two quarter berths. But the vessel was fairly dangerous at sea. We were almost upset in a cross wash outside Bedwell Harbour." A 24-foot Riviera Star added such comforts as a head, a stove and a table with a B.C. chart laminated into it. It also had a "pop-top" so that people could stand up straight when below. When the cabin was "popped", however, it was so high that scrambling to the bow for sail changing was tough.

However, as happens in many a family living on the coast, sailing also led to discord. As Joan wrote in a magazine article ("By Car & By Boat, By Golly!"): "Unlike most husbands and wives, it is I who love sailing, Denis who hates it. When we went for weekends, he always wanted to turn on the motor. 'Let's get there, for Pete's sake, this tacking back and forth is pointless.' How to explain to a frustrated powerboat man that it's the journey, not the arrival that matters?" They overcame B.C.'s irritating, fickle winds by buying his and her boats. Denis purchased a 24-foot Bayliner, *Soul Search*, but sold her after a season, judging that one hole in the water sucking down money was enough. Their next compromise allowed Joan to sail solo to harbours while Denis, staying in touch on the CB radio, would wave fervently to the arriving *EB* after having transported himself to the marina in his first love — the automobile — for gin and tonics, dinner and a sleepover.

During these years, Joan's Austen-Leigh legacy and her 20th-century self continued their intertwining roles. In the mid-1970s, she earned a BA from the University of Victoria, followed by a master's in playwriting from the University of British Columbia.

Between 1967 and 1983, she published 30 plays that have been performed on stage and on radio in Canada, the U.S., the U.K. and Australia. In 1979, at the age of 59, when some people might contemplate resting on their oars, Joan cracked on the sails instead. She published *Stephanie*, her first novel and a bestseller. The same year, she co-founded the Jane Austen Society of North America which, with nearly 4,000 members today, is one of the world's largest literary societies. And she bought *Elizabeth Bennet* (named after Jane Austen's best-known heroine), her refuge, sailing delight and "cottage," on which some of her best adventures took place.

After Joan was widowed in the mid-1980s, she continued writing and sailing. "I'm basically an island hopper," she says. "But I've gone as far as Desolation Sound with its wonderful name and the huge mountains falling straight into the sea. I adored the quaintness of its anchorages and the cinnamon buns we bought at a shack on Cortes Island."

Joan chronicled some of her sailing adventures in *Pacific Yachting*, including one tale in which, spanking along solo near Swartz Bay and trying to listen to "Saturday Afternoon at the Opera," she miscalculated the current, hit a rock, badly cut her head, waited for the tide to float her off, sailed back to town and drove to a clinic to get stitched up. She was only in her late 70s, after all.

Joan laughs remembering pulling into crowded Powell River, with her friend Elspeth on the bow ready to drop anchor, when some "disagreeable" woman said loudly across the water, "The woman always gets to do the dirty work." "Then she saw me," says Joan, "and her jaw dropped. We had a great chuckle over that one."

Then there was the time near San Juan Island's Roche Harbor, when a long line of battleships completely blocked *EB*'s entrance to San Juan Channel. A police boat addressed Joan on a big loudspeaker: "Little sailboat, pass between ships four and five." Although fearful of being rammed, Joan managed to slip *EB* between the behemoths. Joan also guiltily recalls a near collision with a Washington State ferry: "A girlfriend and I were on the poop on the way to Otter Bay. We were busy chatting and not paying proper attention. Suddenly the ferry passed by slowly but very close. We shivered with fear. But the captain radioed us, 'Little boat, sit tight. You'll be alright.' That was a relief! Very friendly, those Washington State ferries."

Joan was also fond of Moby's Marina and Pub in Ganges on Saltspring Island. "I used to sail to Ganges and write there," she recalls. "I'd take my laptop and printer and just write. My last novel, *Invitation to the Party* (2001), was written mostly on the boat. A boat gives you licence. You can paint a picture, do a crossword. A boat demands steak and pancakes and cinnamon buns and doughnuts, all those things you're not allowed at home. Yet I'd like to think I got much done. The fact that one has gone away to write makes one obliged to do so."

In the spring of 2001, Goucher College in Baltimore, home to the world's largest collection of Jane Austen artifacts, awarded Joan an honorary Doctor of Letters for her writings and for her work keeping Jane Austen's legacy alive. The same year, Joan doused *EB*'s sails and turned her boat into a cottage. "I could no longer land the boat by myself. Jumping ashore with lines in my hand was too difficult." But entertaining aboard buoys her spirits. As novelist Carol Shields says, "Joan has a gift for hospitality and takes the same delight in invitations as 'aunt' Jane Austen did. Joan would have fit right into the 18th century."

Yet Joan took full advantage of the 21st: her entertaining went well beyond offering hard tack aboard. "I cooked in advance and had people to dinner on the boat when it was moored in Brentwood Bay. We had lots of gin and tonics and did things we're not supposed to do. We all sat close together, no formalities, no front door, no hanging up of coats. It promotes friendship and conversation. I just love it. I've never been happier than when I've been on the water."

Joan Austen-Leigh/Joan Mason Hurley died between the time she was interviewed and the publication of this book.

racers
and cruisers

Solo Sailing the Five Capes
Around and Around the Island
From Salvaged Skiffs to Galley Proofs
No Time to Waste

Karen Thorndike
solo sailing the five capes

When Karen Thorndike sailed into Hobart, Tasmania, she was greeted as a hero. She'd just completed the longest leg — 96 days — of her world circumnavigation. Suddenly, well-wishers showed up, clinging to her like barnacles to an unpainted bottom. Relishing the warm reception extended by locals, yachties, politicians and reporters, Karen felt deep satisfaction that, at last, people were taking her seriously, that her goal of entering the *Guinness Book of Records* wasn't a menopausal delusion. For Karen wasn't a sailing wife, or a 20-something looking for adventure, but a mid-50s woman aiming to become the first American female to sail solo around five capes: a woman who'd not set foot on a sailboat before age 39; a woman many had dismissed as a dreamer.

When I meet Karen on *Amelia*, the faithful steed that carried her around the globe, her framed Guinness certificate is screwed to a bulkhead. The 36-foot Rival, a fibreglass yacht built in Great Britain, is loaded with gear; her backup, re-stitched sails are stacked on a settee. Karen is short, with Renaissance curves, cheerful blue eyes and blond ringlets, and her stature makes you wonder how she continuously hoisted and lowered sails, reefed, climbed the mast, made repairs and checked and rechecked the rigging and gear. While performing these tasks, she also cooked, ate, slept, kept watch, bathed, did laundry, dried rain- and sea-soaked clothing, ensured the batteries were charged, wrote e-mails and eternally watched the barometer to divine the weather ahead. Her months were punctuated by squalls, gales and storms. Reading her logs gives clear answers to a common question: just what do bluewater sailors *do* while crossing oceans?

When Karen left San Diego on August 4, 1996, she estimated her 33,000-mile journey would take about nine months. When she triumphantly re-moored *Amelia* at the San Diego Yacht Club, two years and two weeks had passed. Why did the circumnavigation take almost three times as long? Karen's adventures show that, like the old sailing ships of yore, once we set sail and leave the confines of our scheduled, controlled and time-restricted lives, the sea, wind and waves take charge and impose the timeline.

The first part of her voyage — San Diego to Hilo, Hawaii — took 23 days. Before leaving, Karen had created a website, and through her laptop and Inmarsat C System she sent and received messages each day, weather permitting. Friends and schoolchildren from around the world monitored her electronic logs, asked questions and sent encouragement. The electromagnetic waves often comforted Karen when she confronted mammoth watery waves and helped her cope with the loneliness of solo sailing. The log also reveals Karen's self-deprecating humour and occasional wry turn of phrase. Instead of telling readers "It's grey and drizzly," she writes: "There's no danger of getting sunburned." She dubs the flying fish expiring on her deck "high seas road kill." She explains that the GPS, which tells her where she is, does not stand for "grey plastic sextant." But the log also demonstrates that offshore sailing can be most unglamorous. During the first leg, her transmission acted up, requiring serious repairs in Hilo. She had a "strange encounter" with a freighter (she calls them "BOSS," for "Big Oncoming Steel Ship"), which altered course to parallel hers and then stopped to watch her sail away without responding to her radio calls. The Aries windvane kept disconnecting. Conflicting winds "battled over the same piece of ocean creating crummy nights."

After the transmission was repaired and Karen received a Hawaiian blessing bestowing "way good luck," she spent four weeks sailing to Papeete in Tahiti. She had the usual problems of lumpy seas, nasty swells, a failing water pump and a seized exhaust valve, and she discovered what it meant to be in the doldrums. She marvelled at the flinty sharpness of tiny salt grains. "I swear the stuff could scratch diamonds." Crossing the equator earned her the designation "shellback." Then, delighted, she found "French bread, French wine and French perfume" at the Papeete quay.

Rounding Cape Horn was next, and Karen vowed to revive the ancient maritime custom of installing a single earring to commemorate the event. She arrived in the Falkland Islands 58 days after lifting anchor in Tahiti. During that two-month passage, Karen realized that "solitude is a great place to visit but not to stay." Her log relates the day-to-day survival issues of bluewater passages — including many days of 35-plus-knot winds — although her funny bone pops up regularly. In the horse latitudes (between 25° and 35° north and south where, because of freshwater shortages, sailing ships once tossed livestock overboard), she reports she hasn't had to "throw any horses overboard yet but they're getting on my nerves."

Port Stanley in the Falklands, an overseas territory of the United Kingdom, is perhaps the only place on earth where windmills could provide all the electricity needed. The winds blast continually, and even moored boats are often tossed around, so Karen used 10 lines to secure *Amelia* to the dock. But she saw penguins, pierced her left earlobe and met "amazingly kind and generous" people. Getting ready for the next, and longest, leg across the wild Indian Ocean required repairs, recaulking and new gaskets. While working on the boat and provisioning for the months to come, Karen wondered which among her "mouldy clothes" she could wear after receiving a dinner invitation to the governor's house.

Karen departed the Falklands on January 29, 1997, in the middle of the southern hemisphere's summer and ran smack into trouble. In those latitudes (about 51°S), summer doesn't mean warm weather or fair winds. Karen had caught a "touch of the flu" in Port Stanley, and as the anemometer readings climbed, so did her temperature. Endlessly buffeted by 50-plus-knot winds, 20-foot waves, rain and lightning, Karen became extremely fatigued and dehydrated. In her log, she wrote, "A potent storm was forecast for February 2 and when it hit, I had not eaten for four days and had slept very little. The storm struck hard and fast, and within the hour, built to 50 knots. I stopped looking at the wind meter when it hit 60 knots. My storm jib wasn't small enough to use as a steering sail and I had to hand steer through the worst of winds and seas. It rained so hard it hurt. With bare poles, the boat averaged eight to nine knots. I'd get the steering set and go below and soon *Amelia* would lose control and go broadside into the waves. I'd dash on deck and get her downwind again. At one point, I experienced terrible chest pains and feared I was having a heart attack. Combined with fatigue, I didn't think I'd live through it so sent a distress call by Comsat e-mail to [her friend] John Oman in Seattle."

Karen was lucky. She was still close enough to the Falklands that escape from her predicament was possible. John Oman immediately tried to telephone the Falklands. The storm had knocked out the lines and he was unable to get through, so he called the United Kingdom Coast Guard. Thus, shortly after Karen's SOS, the HMS *Norfolk* received the search-and-rescue notice. The 400-foot British Duke Class missile frigate was 250 miles south of *Amelia* and steamed toward her at 22 knots while maintaining contact with John Oman, who received updates from Karen every two hours. The next morning, the frigate reached the sailboat. Karen gratefully watched the tender coming across, with three men and one woman "to pluck me off at great risk to themselves. They all faced danger as the small sea boat and *Amelia* were crashing into each other during the rescue." She explains that sailors should be wary of asking for help because it often puts the rescuers at risk. "But," she grins, "should such an unfortunate situation occur, I highly recommend being close to a British navy vessel."

Although safely aboard the frigate, Karen fretted about *Amelia*'s fate. "I'd been told," she recalls, "that if I couldn't return to the yacht, and if the volunteers couldn't sail her back for me, the *Norfolk* would be obliged to sink her." Captain Peter Hudson, after receiving permission from the British government, asked for volunteers to sail *Amelia* back to Port Stanley. Forty offered — four went aboard to rescue the vessel, while the *Norfolk* delivered Karen to the Falklands. There she was diagnosed as having angina pectoris, a condition that triggers severe chest pains when blood flow to the heart is restricted. Karen flew to Seattle for medical treatment and recovery.

Six weeks later, she returned. "I badly wanted to leave the Falklands. The season was sliding into fall, and at those latitudes, it was already snowing, the winds just howled and there were only semi-good places to tie up. Some folks recommended I go to Uruguay. But a friend advised me to winter in Argentina, and in the end I went there, to Mar del Plata. It was a great place and the people were wonderful." After spending nearly six months in that city, Karen left for Tasmania on November 1, 1997, a 96-day voyage during which she passed the next three capes: Cape of Good Hope, Cape Leeuwin south of Perth, Australia, and South East Cape in Tasmania. She experienced bigger storms than those off the Falklands; worried about her cockleshell in the vast ocean, but enjoyed the albatrosses, petrels, dolphins and bioluminescent krill; changed her sails incessantly; grew bored with her canned beans. She vowed her next circumnavigation would not be solo.

Karen did not grow up to be a sailor. Although her dad had a keen interest in things marine, his health kept him off boats. In the early 1960s, Karen enrolled at the University of Washington to study marine biology and communications. She also wanted to be a photographer but found the cost of professional equipment beyond her reach. After learning to work with film, she edited a weekly ski show for several years, experience that eventually led to her becoming a film editor and negative cutter. She's also held positions as a script continuity supervisor and has worked for television shows like "The Fugitive" and "Northern Exposure." During her off hours, she favoured hiking and climbing, scaling mountains like Rainier and Baker. But one day, after a long tramp near Cape Scott on Vancouver Island, she crested a hill and peered down into a cove, where a white gleaming yacht swung at anchor. "Gee," she murmured to herself, "there are better ways of getting here." This small epiphany changed her life.

She signed up for sailing lessons with Seattle Wind Works, then crewed on other people's boats, racing evenings and weekends. She participated in Swiftsure races and was a member of the first all-female crew entering the Victoria-Maui International Yacht Race. She got still more offshore experience bringing boats back from Hawaii. "I've scraped and painted my share of bottoms too," she laughs. "For me, sailing is like a disease for which I haven't found a cure. The old-time sailors had a saying, 'It's easier to swallow the anchor than to turn your back upon the ocean.'"

Karen's apprenticeship lasted a dozen years. She put off buying a boat of her own until she had a specific voyage in mind. "I wanted one true adventure in my life and I wanted it to be sailing. But it was hard financially — I just didn't have enough money and didn't know what kind of boat I wanted." But she was unwavering in her goal. She bought a historic building in Snohomish, renovated and sold it. Profits in the bank, she began shopping for a boat in 1994, telling yacht brokers she desired a 36- to 38-foot boat, preferably steel, but fibreglass might serve. Not wood. "They probably get a lot of people saying, 'Oh, I'm looking for a boat to single-hand around the world.' They all looked at me and said 'Sure, sure,' and never asked me about my experience. They patronized me: everyone knows women can't sail, don't like to sail. Without exception, these brokers showed me just the boats in their inventory, ones that were totally inappropriate, too big, or with huge windows. 'This is the perfect boat for you and your boyfriend or husband, blah, blah, blah.' They really didn't take me seriously." Karen juts out her chin when remembering their condescending manner – she has not forgiven them.

Then, almost accidentally, she found the Rival cutter for sale at Shilshole, a boat with 40,000 offshore miles under her bottom without having developed stress cracks. Karen renamed her *Amelia*, after the intrepid Earhart. She changed the rigging, loaded five anchors, added a life raft and EPIRB (Emergency Position Indicating Radio Beacon), stowed over 300 paper charts and ordered an additional set of sails. She did not make changes to accommodate her size or female strength. "My only problem was that the previous owner, at six foot four, had set the mast steps for his long legs, but I thought, 'Hey, how many times will I have to climb the mast?'" (Several times, it turned out.) She tried to get insurance, but despite her four trips to Hawaii and the 10 deliveries back, she was deemed uninsurable. "Many magazine editors — especially the men — said I would never make it."

When she reached Tasmania, any public doubts about her capability and persistence had vanished. She stayed six weeks, enjoying the Hobartians' intense interest in sailing, recuperating from the three-month solo sail, repairing the windvane and tending to the engine. After passing South West Cape, the fifth and last on her circuit, she arrived in tranquil Dunedin on New Zealand's South Island. From Dunedin, she sailed east, staying between 35° and 40°S, and then turned north to Tahiti, arriving 30 days later. After weeks of eating out of tins, she delighted in dining at the "roulottes" selling pizza, Chinese food, *steak-frites* and crepes. She felt quite at home nearly four weeks later, disembarking again in Hilo, Hawaii, a place where she could easily repair the roller furling that had split. To set the Guinness record, one last passage — Hilo to San Diego — awaited her. Birds resting aboard, much floating debris and several cockroach families kept Karen company. As always, her humour sparkled: "At least the cucarachas are the small ones and not the giant kind that move the furniture." The winds were light, so Karen moved slowly, taking 35 days to reach San Diego, a city that proclaimed "Karen Thorndike Day, First American Woman to Circumnavigate the Globe," after she arrived. The cities of Coronado, Port Angeles and Snohomish also instituted a Karen Thorndike Day. Many other honours followed, including being named *Seattle Post-Intelligencer* Sports Star of the Year and winning the Cruising Club of America's Blue Water Sailing and 1998 Circumnavigation Awards.

Since her return to Seattle, Karen has resumed her film-editing career, but the global sail still influences her life. "I am more at peace and satisfied. I don't feel a need to prove myself to others. I wish I'd experienced that complete solitude long ago because it makes you search inside yourself and resolve what's truly important in your life." She's co-authoring a book called *Yes I Can* about her experiences. She speaks to kids, Rotary Clubs and conferences about the psychology of achieving. She's keeping the boat and dreams of sailing to South Georgia near the Antarctic Circle — maybe this time with a man who understands engines. "If only I were 30," she sighs, "I'd be gone in a flash.

"When you first go offshore, you're afraid. I was afraid of the southern ocean storms. During those first storms I was overwhelmed with fear, wondering what would happen to my poor old boat. When big waves crash against you, it sounds like freight trains ram the yacht. It's totally shocking. But then I'd lean back in the cockpit and get that sense of wonder. The feeling I was a guest, floating in a world that no one owns, a world I was privileged to experience."

Dick Pattinson
around and around
the Island

Dick Pattinson leaps up and, at a speed belying his 86 years, darts outside, air horn in hand. He lets out three sharp blasts. A swiftly sailing American yacht tacks in time to avoid a submerged killer rock lurking in front of Dick's house on Ganges Harbour, Saltspring Island. He comes back satisfied. "Happens quite often," he beams, light blue eyes twinkling behind his steel-framed glasses. "Skippers are busy trimming their sails and forget to look at the chart."

Comfortably seated in the cozy home Dick shares with Christina, his wife of 62 years, we've been poring over the photo album depicting his 13th circumnavigation of Vancouver Island, a voyage he completed in the summer of 2002. Before he begins telling me about his voyages, Dick has shown me his behind-the-garage workshop, its shelves piled high with old ships' radios, antennas, electronic gear and tools. Dick was a vital part of the radio revolution that brought news and communications to fishing boats, trading ships, isolated logging camps, canneries, homesteaders and lighthouses scattered among British Columbia's islands and inlets. These radios have dominated his life, allowed him to travel huge sections of B.C.'s coast and, indirectly, turned him into a sailor.

A modest man, Dick tells his story without fanfare. Born in the Vancouver suburb of Burnaby, he attended King Edward High School, which offered training in radios. "My mother suggested I learn radios," says Dick, "saying it'd allow me to serve 'above the waterline' on ships." However, after Dick obtained his radio operator's licence, he only made a single boat trip: on the Union Steamship *Cardena*. "I replaced the wireless Morse code operator during the Christmas run to Prince Rupert in northern B.C. It was wonderful being on that ship. I would have liked to have done more voyages like that, lots more."

In 1937, he took his first full-time job operating and servicing the radios for Nelson Brothers Fisheries, a pilchard cannery in Nootka Sound on the Pacific. Rumours of war made radio jobs more plentiful, so he moved on to Yellowknife in the Northwest Territories to build a network for Consolidated Mining and Smelting. Then, when Canada entered World War II in 1939, telecommunications innovator Donald Hings recruited Dick to Ottawa, where he was involved in building C-18 sets and other, smaller radios. "I tried to enlist," recalls Dick, "but Don said, 'If we're in the army, they'll tell us how to build radios. It won't work.'" So Dick continued his top-secret defence work ("I call it 'offence' work," he laughs) until "the Germans surrendered." Five years in Ottawa were enough. Because of his love for the west coast, he applied for a Department of Transport job in Alert Bay, again operating radios.

But after six months, his entrepreneurial instincts kicked in. "I could repair radios on fishing boats and be my own boss," he says. "This was before VHF. It was quite a luxury to have radios on boats, but as time went on, the fishermen got more equipment. I even manufactured radios of my own ... that red case up there is one of them."

Initially, he competed with Jim Spilsbury, the famous radio pioneer who founded Spilsbury and Tindall Radio Communications. "But," says Dick, "I was a one-man show and I found it was more profitable to sell their sets than to tie up my time manufacturing my own design. I also had the agencies for other makes — Marconi, Daniels, Apelco, Bendix, Decca Radar and Ekolite Sounders."

Servicing radios and electronics became Dick's livelihood for 33 years. He moved through the high frequency revolution. "They invented new radio tubes every year. They failed frequently so I had to carry a large assortment of tubes to repair radios on seiners and gillnetters, and in fishing lodges and logging camps. Later we moved on to transistors."

To get to the boats quickly and prevent them from losing fishing time, he chartered seaplanes, but he never knew how long repairs would take — five minutes or five hours — and the plane and its pilot would be sitting there, waiting, racking up the fees. It made him — and his cost-conscious clients — ill at ease, so in 1957, he bought his own seaplane, which he piloted for the next 19 years. "Clients paid the airplane's costs, but I could travel fast and didn't have to charge for time the plane was idle during the repair job."

Dick viewed the seaplane much like a car. "The sea was the road. I liked flying and hated to give it up, but I sold the aircraft in 1975. I think I stopped in time. In a plane, you only need to make one mistake." Nevertheless, he recalls one tale about a passenger who thought Dick a bit reckless. He'd picked up a German fellow at Nimpkish Lake one late Friday afternoon. "I flew to Alert Bay, side-slipped over the cannery and landed. To me it was business as usual, but to my passenger it was terrifying. He was kind of shaken and said, 'Tit you fly in de last var?' He probably thought I was getting back at him somehow."

With the plane sold, personal boats entered Dick's life. His first was a small runabout with a one-cylinder Vivian. He then bought a 24-foot powerboat, but in 1977 he retired to Saltspring and joined the sailing club. "The price of fuel was rising and the boat was hungry for it. It'd go about 20 knots. Then this sailboat, a Grampian 26, came on the market. I bought 'er, renamed her *Gwaihir* and sold the powerboat. Never looked back, really."

So at 65, when most people focus on collecting their pension, Dick began his sailing career. "I'd been flying, you know, and that depends on the wind too. I understood the principles of it. The sailboat had a dandy big genoa and I won a few races with it. But after that sail wore out, well, I was sailing yesterday and I came in at my usual spot — last. All the other boats have spinnakers. But I don't want to get involved in that. Too much trouble."

His first trip around Vancouver Island occurred in 1983. Not wanting to single-hand, he collected a lengthy list of people who volunteered to accompany him. "But in the end, only one fellow, Jack Hoadley, older than I was, came along. It's always the same. Many volunteer, few turn up. Now about half the ones who signed up in the early days are gone. One time I went around solo but had a buddy boat as company."

Dick remembers a fellow he took as crew who "just couldn't wait to get back from the west coast to pick his raspberries. 'Raspberries?' I asked him. 'Here you're having this unique experience on this wild coast and you worry about raspberries?'" He chuckles at the recollection and the absurdity of the fellow's desire.

Some of his companions travel only portions of the trip. In 2002, Bernard Kruel, a friend of Dick's son (a youngster of only about 55), joined the voyage in Port Hardy and stayed for three weeks. "He was a great cook and brought a satchel of condiments." Others have been fishermen, regularly putting a nice salmon on the table.

But it's not all been fun. His 2000 adventure was plagued by a failing engine. While he was circumnavigating with companion Harold Brochmann, the Yanmar began squirting water out of the air intake. Six days in Schooner Cove and a monster repair bill later, the pair chugged around the island, afraid to turn off the engine for fear it would never start again. Dick was so frustrated he replaced the balky contraption with a brand-new one.

Thirteen times around Vancouver Island. With the side trips and seeking anchorages, each voyage is about 700 nautical miles. Why does he keep on doing it? "I haven't seen it all yet. And there are places I like to go back to." Dick spends anywhere from 20 to 34 days circling the island, anchoring out at night. His itinerary varies, but his usual haunts include Schooner Cove, Comox, Kanish Bay, Forward Harbour, Port Neville, Alert Bay, Port Hardy and Bull Harbour on the Inside Passage. On the Pacific coast, he visits Sea Otter Cove, Winter Harbour, Klaskish Inlet, Columbia Cove, Kyuquot, Queens Cove, Friendly Cove, Hot Springs Cove, Tofino, Ucluelet, Bamfield, Port Renfrew and Sooke.

Dick loves exploring and uncovering the unusual. "In one empty village, I found a big totem pole, face down, and a tree I estimate to be at least 70 years old growing through it — its roots tangling around it. I also visit a burial island just out from Battle Bay, where I see the decaying remnants of a dugout canoe. Three skulls sit on top of it and each year they're mossier. These are the kind of experiences that make it interesting for me."

He's been intrigued for years by a mystery, told to him by an old fisherman, about a U.S. bomber that crash-landed during World War II between Winter Harbour and Cape Cook. The fisherman found the bodies sitting around a dead campfire some months later. Their dog tags were gone. Who removed the tags? Why did the airmen starve with seafood available with each tidal change? Dick would like to unravel their secret one day.

His favourite spot is Columbia Cove. "You can go up the little inlet there and hike for 30 minutes to this splendid beach. It's usually deserted. The things that drift in are remarkable, although the Japanese glass floats have mostly disappeared. One year I found a weather buoy. Figured it was valuable and called the Coast Guard. But it's still there."

His two decades of cruising around the island also record the changes taking place. He's seen hillsides where forests were cut to the ground now covered with new growth. He's seen the fishing fleet dwindle, canneries disappear and docks fall down. "Winter Harbour, once a really active fishing port, now has weeds growing through the wharf," he says sadly.

Dick has been a ham radio operator since 1934, and during his circumnavigations he calls home on the single sideband so his wife can listen to his reports on his whereabouts. Usually he communicates by voice, but recently in Hot Springs Cove, when it was time for his radio sked with a buddy, Dick had to switch to the Morse code he learned more than 60 years ago. "The engine noise kept me from hearing the voice, so I quickly looked for my transmitter key. Couldn't find the darn thing. So I whistled code into the microphone. And they answered in key code. Just like the old days." He guffaws at the recollection.

His trips around Vancouver Island are meticulously recorded. Each journey is listed on a spreadsheet, with precise locations and dates. Thirteen albums, one for each voyage, display superb photos with captions marking dates and places. Leafing through, I note how Dick's artistic eye highlights a few longhouse supports decaying in an abandoned native village, the slanting sun illuminating the corner of a lonely cove, a decaying cannery in Nootka, a stunning sunset.

What inspires an 86-year-old to keep travelling those 700 miles – a venture that many people half his age find too demanding? "Why shouldn't I?" he laughs. "It's a lot of fun. I like to go. You must enjoy life while you got it." Will there be a 14th trip? Not according to Dick, who thinks the last voyage was enough. Although he admits he might like to spend a bit more time out there, or see some more of the Broughton Archipelago. His wife reminds him that every year has been his last, and when spring rolls around ...

Gwaihir, named after the Lord of the Wind in Tolkien's *Lord of the Rings*, is distinctive. If you see a grass-green, 26-foot, 26-year-old Grampian around Vancouver Island, I recommend you follow in her wake. Her skipper knows the history, hidey-holes and First Nations' sites on this coast. Besides, we could all use a buddy boat.

Ole Hansen
from salvaged skiffs to galley proofs

A carved, painted panel graces the dining room wall in Ole Hansen's house overlooking Puget Sound in Edmonds, Washington; it depicts a stylized, almost primitive, scene of sailors rowing a whaling skiff against foamy waves, and a brawny whaler on the bow preparing to hurl a heavy harpoon. Ahead of the whaler, stark white with a plume spouting from its blowhole, Moby Dick has a mocking look on its face. The *Pequod*, in full sail, hovers on the horizon. A huge flying albatross gives the tableau a melancholy touch. The scene is powerful, elemental, a contest of man against nature.

The panel once formed the front of Ole Hansen's toy box, built, carved and painted by his artist father, Armin Hansen. Throughout his childhood, Ole looked at this salty scene, unconsciously absorbing the message — the muscle, the daring, Ahab's obsession. Armin Hansen spent a good part of his life on all manner of ships (in part to put "bacon and beans on the table" during the Depression), and most of his highly collectible paintings and etchings focus on marine subjects. "My father was a great talker and routinely told us tales of his nautical adventures," says Ole. "Yet he never encouraged me to go to sea. On the contrary. He put me on a fish boat with an old salt when I was just a bit of a twerp, hoping I'd get deathly seasick and would lose any affection I might have for those damn boats." Armin's ploy backfired. Ole never suffered seasickness and the ocean's breakers persistently beat their siren song. Throughout his growing years, he joined old-timer commercial fishermen on their ocean foraging.

Ole was "hatched" in 1924 in Monterey, California, once the capital of the Spanish territory of Alta California and later the setting for John Steinbeck's *Cannery Row*. The sea was omnipresent. When he grew a bit older, he and his friends "took mussels off the rocks, smashed them for bait, put a meaty hunk on a hook and in no time, you'd have a fish." During the Depression, yachts were rare, and even dinghies were beyond most people's means, but Ole took advantage of the northeasters sweeping into Monterey Bay. After big storms, skiffs that had "busted their moorings" would litter beaches. "My friends and I often walked among the wreckage, found something we could have fun with, hauled it clear of the debris and placed a one-line ad in the *Monterey Herald*: 'Found, skiff, identify.' If no one called, it was ours. We knew how to bang it back together (my dad gave me my own little tool chest when I was seven), nailing leeboards on the side, cutting a pine pole for the mast, carving oars and sewing up some canvas lying around the basement. This is how we'd get us a boat. It was rough-and-ready sailing and we'd go out and bust 'er up in the surf. It's a wonder we survived because if you came off the top of a breaker and she stuck her nose into the sand, there was wood splintering in all directions."

Ole is still a bear of a man at six foot four inches (he says he's shrunk a bit now that he's in his 70s), and he's lost most of his hair; his kind blue eyes grow humid when he recounts his past exploits using his droll, colourful turns of phrase. Without a doubt, he undertook adventures that would horrify today's parents. No one drove Ole to school or anywhere else in a black Model-T, the SUV of the day. From the age of 13 on, he'd spend summers taking the bus and then tramping the Santa Lucia Mountains with his little rifle and some fishing gear — at times alone, sometimes with a buddy. "Before I left the house my father would stick a handful of sausage in my pocket just in case I was gone for a week or more."

In 1942, Ole enlisted in the navy. In those days, a recruit needed to present three letters of recommendation to be accepted. That was when Ole's heritage caught up with him. Harking back to the family's Danish origins, his parents had christened him "Wendelborg" Hansen. Aware that word might not trip easily off American tongues, they nicknamed their son "Mötje," a name used throughout his school years. (I asked Ole if these two difficult monikers led to teasing at school. If they did, it never bothered him.) When Ole appeared at the navy draft office with his reference letters, they referred to the eager 17-year-old enlistee as "Wendelborg," "Mötje" and "W.M." Hansen. "Who are all these guys?" the puzzled recruiter asked. "They're all me," Ole responded. "And this is how I got to be Ole," he laughs, his ruddy cheeks quivering. "The navy gave me a choice, 'Ole' or 'Swede.' You can see what I chose."

Besides changing his name, the navy decided to transform the recruit into "an officer and a gentleman" and sent him to various schools. The one he remembers best is Missouri Valley College, located directly across the street from the home of Ann, the woman who became his "girl" for life, and with whom, after 55 years of marriage, he's still deeply in love. A New Jersey training camp, Columbia University and torpedo school followed. Ole, eager for action, was frustrated. "All this time I'm supposed to be looking for Japanese ships. I barely managed to survive the training." By the time he was assigned to a 1,630-ton Benson Class destroyer in Norfolk, Virginia, the European war was over. "We were getting ready for the shindig in Japan when Harry dropped the big egg." After non-stop order changes and some time "knocking up and down the Atlantic coast," Ole demobbed and returned to Monterey.

Taking advantage of the GI Bill, he attended the University of California at Berkeley, where he "majored in diploma." Along the way, he and Ann "got spliced." He earned a business degree ("I can't imagine anyone less business administrated than me," he jokes), then worked at several jobs until he settled into representing Armstrong Brothers Tool Company, covering a territory from Oregon through Saskatchewan. The family — a daughter and son had been born to Ann and Ole — moved to Edmonds, just north of Seattle, happy to remain near the water. They acquired *Rumplestiltskin*, a 13-foot runabout with a 15-horsepower Evinrude, which took them all over Puget Sound and the San Juan and Gulf islands. "We'd throw in our sleeping bags, launch the boat somewhere and take off. Sometimes we'd go for a week or two; we slept on the beach at places like Sidney Spit and all kinds of other nifty spots. As the kids grew, we got a somewhat bigger boat with a cuddy cabin."

But Ole still hankered to be the skipper of a boat, so in 1962, he ordered a 37-foot Atkins North Sea pilot ketch, "with a canoe stern and a little 12-horse in her," from Tom Taylor's Vancouver boatyard and, after the hull was completed, finished the interior himself. He met the renowned sailors Miles and Beryl Smeeton and John Guzzwell, who further inspired him to pursue an offshore voyage. "We built *Tangeroa*, named after the Polynesian god of the sea, with the South Pacific trip in mind. It was my carrot in front of the donkey's nose." And only a wooden boat would do. "Damn right," he says emphatically. "I can fix a wooden boat anywhere in the world. Just give me an axe and a tree. A glass boat I'm not so sure. There's much to be said for them, but they don't talk to me very well." Finally the family was ready to go. "And by golly," says Ole, "my final paycheque came and other money rained on us. It was the damnedest thing I ever saw. Things I didn't even know about, the retirement fund and profit-sharing plan and, boy, suddenly it wasn't as hard as I thought it was going to be. We sold the house, put things in storage and took off."

Using a sextant and a "big old Hamilton hack watch that looked like an old railroad turnip," the family navigated to French Polynesia and for the next 18 months meandered through the Marquesas and Tuamotus. While today, hundreds of boats pass through these archipelagos each season, in 1964, cruising yachts were rare. Hearing about the throngs now sailing these waters, Ole recalls visiting Ua Huka's Vaipaee. "They thought they were being overrun by boats because, by golly, there was one through there just three years before." By the time they visited Tahiti, like many parents cruising with kids, they grew worried about their children's schooling. Their daughter, Karyl, 14, breezed through her correspondence homework, but 10-year-old Dirk, who "saw things upside down and sideways," was stymied. Ole explains that no one knew about dyslexia in those days and that the tension around schoolwork was ruining things for everyone. "Finally, we told Dirk to forget about the goddamn books, for him to have a good time and catch up when we get back. That's what happened. He graduated from high school and works happily as a boat builder." The family returned to Edmonds in the fall of 1965, looking to re-establish life ashore.

Ole recounts how he and Tom Kincaid — also at an employment crossroad — sat on the floor one night, wondering "how the hell we were going to feed the kids." Tom, who'd worked as a journalist, suggested starting a little boating newspaper. The idea appealed to Ole: it was a job that would continue to connect him to the sea. After analyzing the market and noting there was no boating publication in the Pacific Northwest, they decided to take a crack at publishing. They chatted with a banker friend, who told them to be prepared for five years of escalating debt — the entrepreneurs had to break even in the first two months. Despite the banker's gloomy forecast, the resolute duo published the first issue of *Nor'westing* in October 1965. "We'd designed it as a tab newspaper and printed it on book stock. We ran something like 5,000 spoils before the press operators figured out how to run that kind of paper. God, it was a disaster. But we finally had enough for a mailing."

Marketing the new boating magazine was tricky. Regional yacht club members became the first target for subscriptions. "All it takes is a couple of clams," an ad proclaimed. Subscribers took them at their word and clams poured through the mail slot. The U.S. Postal Service delivered clams wrapped in shoe boxes and myriad other packaging. "We honoured the subscriptions of those who sent in the smelly things. We did all kinds of things like that and then we gave presentations at the yacht clubs in exchange for our being able to pitch the publication. That's what led to having a paid circulation."

Tom and Ole ran the magazine for nearly three decades. Tom wrote the stories. Ole peddled ad space, took photos ("I'd been a camera nut for years"), developed them, produced half-tones and did page layouts. Even Armin Hansen might have approved this marriage of publishing and boating. They first rented space on the presses of the *Tribune Review*, then switched to their own "Rube Goldberg" linotype machine. They set the type, proofread and pasted up the magazine. Although it was a hand-to-mouth operation for a while, revenue grew sufficiently to support two families.

Noting that August was a sluggish business month, they went cruising, covered the Gulf Islands and the west coast and collected a year's worth of articles and photos from their holiday. Their circulation grew to 10,000, and the dynamic duo eventually bought a powerboat so they could cover the many events up and down the Pacific Northwest coast. Ole, too busy to maintain and sail his *Tangeroa*, put her on the market with great regret. His focus had switched from wooden boats to yachts on paper. He remained with *Nor'westing* for 27 years, when he sold his interest to Tom, whom he still considers his best friend. Often, when the magazine was put to bed, they'd go out for a spin on the "corporate yacht," regardless of the weather. "I've been in some dicey spots with Tom on a boat, but we always ended up sitting down and having a belt together and saying, 'That was a funny one, wasn't it?'"

Over the years, Ole raced and helped deliver boats for others. When a boat needed to be moved, he'd jump at the chance to be out on the water. In this way he sailed from Cape Breton to Maine, from Tortola to Grand Bahama, from the Canary Islands to Barbados. When he was 70, he joined his friend Bob Sylvester, 80, on a Spencer 42 and spent three months exploring Alaska. "Just two old buggers bouncing around Alaska doing their swan song, but we had a grand good time." The last boat delivery took place three years ago. "We were sailing toward the Turks and Caicos Islands in the Caribbean and I could see trouble coming, with easterly flows from the Atlantic blowing like the devil. The rest of the gang was asleep below. I was on watch and realized that we had to get this boat shortened and snugged down when, by God, I realized that I couldn't move quick enough to do it right and had to call for help from down below. That's when I decided to stop going off on deliveries. If I can't pull my weight any longer I have absolutely no damn business being there."

An oxygen bottle accompanies Ole wherever he goes, feeding vital oxygen into his nostrils through clear, thin tubes. He's used his boat skills to make a harness out of webbing so the jug can be carried like a fanny pack. He blames his chronic obstructive pulmonary disease on having dug fine clay out of a basement in his youth, to mucking around in asbestos insulation and to well over three decades of indulging in tobacco. His father introduced him to smoking. "My pa told me the probability was that I was going to smoke, so I might as well start out right and do it at home. I was about 15 when he gave me a pipe. So I smoked and it wasn't any big thing. Pop and I liked trout fishing and while driving to a stream somewhere during the season, I'd roll cigarettes for him. Soon I started rolling them for me. That led to tailor-mades and cigars and I smoked pretty heavily for a long time." One day Ole was waiting to see a *Nor'westing* client and, while reaching for a cigarette, burned his hand on the one already there. He called himself a "stupid bastard and a slave." Without announcing it to anyone, he vowed to quit — and did. That was 25 years ago. "I'm still around," Ole says somewhat wistfully, "but there are so many things that I can't do anymore it drives me nuts. And one of them is being on a boat."

Yet the brine still flows in his veins. In his office, photos of boats and sailors cover the walls; his ditty bag is packed and he's ready to go back on watch. In his exceptionally well-equipped workshop, the walls blanketed with neat rows of clamps and tools of every description, he putters and tinkers and still repairs the occasional nautical bit. He couldn't imagine moving to Arizona and giving up the view of Puget Sound. "Throughout my life, I have been connected to the sea. Even when I supported my family as an equipment salesman, we'd spend weekends on the boat. And all those years with the boating magazine tied me to salt air. Being on the water, I don't know, I just love every bit of it. It teaches you to depend on yourself, not the Coast Guard. You learn self-control in close quarters. You're more observant of what's around. You learn to sort out the guys that are worthwhile. And in a million years, I haven't got enough hands and legs and fingers and toes to count all the worthwhile people I've met through the sea."

Dave Cook
no time to waste

Typically, Olympic sailors are lithe, agile, fast-moving athletes capable of rolltacking in a flash. Dave Cook doesn't fit that stereotype: he travels in a wheelchair. But that does not stalemate him. On the contrary, Dave has raced sailboats competitively for decades, and in Atlanta's 1996 Paralympics tourney, he won a silver medal.

Dave and I talk in his modest, single-family home in Victoria, B.C. Steep steps lead up to the front door. How does Dave get in, I'd wondered while mounting those steps. "My dad installed an elevator for me years ago," explains Dave. "Just a small one that fits my chair and gets me from the drive-in basement to the main floor. In fact, this is my parents' house and except for a couple of years, I've lived here my entire life." The 44-year-old sits very straight, almost motionless, his thick, brushcut hair greying, his clear green eyes lively and young. He shows me how he's remodelled the kitchen for his personal use without making it "institutional." He uses the spacious, under-the-counter drawers for storing food and dishes; a pull-out cutting board serves as countertop. "I deal with my disability partly by not making my environment appear as if I have one."

Dave's condition — "for simplicity's sake, let's just call it 'progressive muscular atrophy'" — was diagnosed when he was 15. After high-school graduation, having learned woodworking from his dad, Dave obtained a job at the Canadian Forces Base in Esquimalt on southern Vancouver Island. It was at the dockyard, surrounded by colleagues who'd grown up in boating families, that Dave caught the sailing bug. "They talked about sailing all the time so I thought I'd give it a whirl. A friend of my dad's, a Royal Victoria Yacht Club member, took me for a sail up to Sidney one day. There was no wind and we motored the whole way, but just being on the water was so tremendous … "

When he was only 18, Dave figured he earned enough to own a boat, and although he'd never sailed, he bought a Cal 20 in Vancouver for $4,000. "She was called *Metaxa*, after that god-awful Greek brandy or whatever it is, terrible stuff." The boat was falling apart, so he went to Vancouver on weekends to make her seaworthy enough to bring back to Victoria. Preliminary repairs made, he and a buddy left Vancouver one afternoon and tied up to the Point Grey log booms overnight to get an early start crossing the Strait of Georgia. "The next morning, halfway across, my friend went below and yelled, 'Dave, take a look, there's a foot of water above the floorboards.' I quickly killed the engine (I didn't know how to put up sails yet) and saw a stream of light piercing the transom. One of the bolts holding the pintle had sheared off. I didn't have any tools with me, so I whipped off a sock and banged it into the hole with a pencil to slow the leak. We bailed and eventually made it back. That was my introduction to sailing. It showed me that I'd better take lessons and learn about boats."

He signed up for a Power and Sail Squadron course and, accompanied by others, practised sailing continually, with Dave responsible for steering ("When we raced, I rarely crewed; my job was always steering"). But he completed one single-handed circumnavigation of San Juan Island. "I wanted to see if I could do it. I sailed downwind between San Juan and Lopez islands with the spinnaker on the foredeck. I'd attached lines to the tiller and the gunwales so I could grab the spinnaker, steer and work the sheets from the foredeck. In retrospect it might've been better to leave it all at the stern, but I guess I wanted to feel the freedom being on the foredeck all by myself with no one steering the boat." Rain poured down as Dave pulled into Friday Harbor where "an older couple invited me to come into their boat for

179

dinner because they felt so sorry for me, soaking wet in this little boat. But I felt really accomplished when I completed the voyage. It felt so good."

The first regatta he entered with *Metaxa* was the Cal 20 fleet championships. "I'd never raced before and didn't know the rules too well, but we didn't come last." More racing followed. Dave gleefully remembers when he bested one of the fellows who'd taught him sailing basics. "After a year of practice I beat this guy in one race and it really pissed him off. He was a lifelong sailor and I was just a rookie." Completely smitten with racing, Dave joined the Canadian Forces Sailing Association and bought a Spencer 28 called *Delicia*. But she was a heavy cruising boat, a "terrible racer," and Dave quickly replaced her with a Curry 25, and then a Hotfoot 27, called *Horizon*. It was Dave's first brand-new boat and he was so thrilled he trailered her to San Diego and participated in the midget ocean racing circuit.

In 1991, Dave's reduced muscle power forced him to begin using a wheelchair. Organized sailing for people with disabilities was off his radar screen until one event changed his mind. "I didn't really accept my disability. I dealt with it but wouldn't accept it. But finally, after I'd thought about it a lot, I entered the 'Shake-a-Leg' race for sailors with disabilities in Newport, Rhode Island. That regatta turned me around mentally. I realized I hadn't wanted to associate with disabled people; I wanted to hang out with other sailors. But sailors with disabilities was completely different: we had an interest in common beyond our disability."

Other events at the regatta also influenced Dave's views about disabled sailing (this is the term used by the International Association for Disabled Sailing and other organizations promoting adaptive sailing). After watching Dave struggle to get out of a car, another participant came over and offered him a transfer board, a 30- by 6-inch, tapered-edge piece of yellow cedar. "It was perfect for me," Dave says, showing me the thin, smooth slab. "It lets me transfer from the wheelchair to anything — a bed, chair or car. It bridges the gap. I put baby powder on it, and rather than lifting myself, I can slide my butt along the wood." That piece of wood inspired Dave to see other adaptations useful to people with disabilities who want to sail. Moreover, he got his first taste of teaching. A competitor able to use only his facial muscles was responsible for calling racing tactics on another sailboat. He approached Dave and asked for help. Each evening of the four-day regatta, Dave and the tactician would meet and strategize. "This sailor was unhappy because his boat was coming in dead last by a mile. He was lousy at tactics and the other people weren't listening to him, but his paralysis didn't allow for any other contribution. The last night we talked strategy really late, and in the next race he beat two boats. It made his day. It also made me feel good because I like to see people master a new skill."

Mastering skills and excelling is crucial to Dave. Calling himself "stubborn," he's quietly persistent about attaining his goals. After the Newport Regatta, thinking he'd only participate once in this type of sailing, he was urged by his friend Kathy Campbell and Bill MacDonald, his boss and commodore of the Canadian Forces Sailing Association, to organize a Paralympic team. Initially, Dave lacked enthusiasm. "But my competitive edge came out and I recruited other sailors with disabilities to enter the Paralympic national eliminations in Toronto. I worked with Ken Kelly and Kirk Westergaard, who still race together and recently competed in the World Sailing Championships in the Netherlands. Canada now has 19 active disabled sailing teams." The competitors raced Laser-designer Bruce Kirby's Sonar 23s, which are specially adapted. Dave's team won every race and earned a spot in the 1996 Atlanta Paralympics, held immediately after the Olympic Games. They won the silver. "We competed on Lake Lanier, a large lake with light and shifty winds. That's what I like, light winds, because in those conditions my lack of mobility is not an issue. I do well in light winds because over the years I've learned to look farther ahead. I sit to windward whenever possible and look up the race course to assess what the winds will do."

Since that exciting win, Dave has been increasingly active in disabled sailing. He explains that three types of boats — the Sonar 23, the 2.4 metre (a one-person keelboat) and the Martin

16s designed by Vancouver's Don Martin — are used most often in the adaptive sailing fleet (all three also serve able-bodied sailors). He's attended events in Florida and Massachusetts. He served as Canadian representative for disabled sailing at the International Sailing Federation meeting held in Sweden, and recently, he flew to Australia to evaluate a new version of the Access Dinghy (an Australian design aimed at qualifying for the Paralympics) and observed two truly inspirational young women. "I watched a 13-year-old girl with only one tiny leg and three toes, but no arms, sailing this boat by herself. The other woman, Nava, who's 21, is paralyzed except for her facial muscles and breathes through a ventilator. She's from the Cook Islands and the sailing gets her out. It's something that she can do on her own. She's never been able to do anything without help. My friend Bob Bentham, who accompanied me to Australia, coached Nava from a Zodiac. There are really inspirational people in this type of adaptive sailing, so being involved kicks me in the ass and tells me, 'Hey I'm not really bad off; there are others with worse problems.'"

Dave has grown immensely interested in devices that can help sailors with disabilities to compete. While serving on the Canadian sailing team, he dreamed up ways to adapt seats, seat belts and railing handholds. "There's been tremendous progress in adaptation mechanisms. We have electrically powered winches, servo-assist controls that allow you to steer a boat by pushing buttons or running a boat by blowing into a tube." Devices, though, are only part of sailing success. He also concentrates on the mental processes of making sailors work together as a team. In the summer of 2002, he raced a Hobie Cat 16 in the Vancouver Waves Regatta, sharing the boat with Seattle-based Peter Nelson. The two had never met before the race, so Dave e-mailed a self-analysis to Peter, outlining his sailing preferences and his strong and weak points. He wrote that he is effective in light winds but hates strong winds, that he pays attention to detail and that he's stubborn. Peter responded with his own preferences and the two avoided surprises and conflicts.

Dave retired from his dockyard job in 1997 when he started using a wheelchair. After signing up for a business management course and buying a computer, he started his own business — a marine mail-order company selling boat parts inexpensively. "The business didn't flourish," Dave says drily, "but I didn't lose any money and learned a skill, so in that sense it was successful." In 1999, he started the Victoria Sailing Foundation, an organization designed to help disadvantaged young people experience the joys of sailing and the freedom of being on the water. The foundation is a registered charity that accepts cash and boats. "We teach the youths to sail, to maintain and to repair the boats, then sell the vessels to cover expenses. We've had about 150 young people participate, but I can count the number of success stories on one hand. The target audience has major social and developmental challenges, kids in difficulty with the law, kids who don't go to regular school because of their behaviour. Unfortunately, only a few keep with it after the novelty wears off. You need to have the passion to keep sailing. And our philosophy is that the youths must participate, work on the boats. Most of them think they've got better things to do with their time, but there are a few who're really keen."

Dave's life is about to change significantly again — indirectly because of sailing. Two years ago, he met New Zealander Raewyn McLean at a THRASH Regatta (a phrase invented by Royal Victoria Yacht Club competitors that stands for "Thank Heavens Racing and Spring Are Here"). The couple plans a wedding in 2003. "It's very exciting because I never thought I would fall in love like I have. I didn't think that kind of life was for me." Newly re-energized, he wants to start a consulting business in inspirational speaking (not motivational speaking, he clarifies). He has already given talks to Rotary Clubs, school groups and youth leadership meetings. "I use my work and sailing experience to talk about overcoming obstacles, enhancing performance, analyzing and identifying strong and weak points, and focussing on improving weak points. It's basically building self-esteem and showing people that no obstacle is too great if you put your mind to it and put in the effort. I'm getting great feedback from my audiences."

He also hopes to do more cruising. He's got a kit bag full of lines and blocks to get himself in and out of boats. "My fiancée and I went away cruising a month ago and she got me up and down the cabin by herself using a block and tackle. There are always ways around obstacles. I believe sailing has given me more opportunities than I could've had with other sports. When I began sailing, I had no idea how beneficial it would be. I learned to problem-solve. On the water, I learned to look ahead at the winds and prepare for what's coming. And I earned respect from people I respect. Sailing has given me the opportunity to find myself and now I can use the things I've learned to motivate other people. I want to share with them that if you put in the effort, there's no storm too strong to stop you."

hot vents,
whales and fish

Explorer of the Hot, Deep Sea
Rock Solid
The Eavesdropper
The Evangelist of Fishing

Verena Tunnicliffe
explorer of the hot, deep sea

"There's nothing like the bottom of the ocean to make you feel completely insignificant and totally maladapted." So begins University of Victoria marine biologist Verena Tunnicliffe, who has first-hand experience with some of the world's hottest undersea sites. The energetic 40-something scientist spends a good part of her life studying the unusual life forms thriving in the oceans at depths of three miles. Using an uncrewed submersible directed by fibre-optic cable from a research ship, Verena has discovered some 70 animal species never identified before — species, moreover, that contradict all our previous understanding of what life needs to survive.

Unlike people who were awestruck by the sea during childhood, Verena grew up in landlocked central Ontario. Then one day her mother, returning from a trip to Florida, brought her daughter a gift: a small wooden box encrusted with shells. Verena was only seven, but this seemingly insignificant present piqued her interest in ocean life — the shells' pretty, varied shapes excited her curiosity and offered a glimpse of a world far away from the Ontario landscape (Verena still has the box in her office). She began looking up the names of the animals that created those shells and, reading about their origins in various books, vowed to become a marine biologist. "Mum collected other shells for me," Verena says, "and I watched Jacques Cousteau's programs. He showed me what was underwater."

She had other support at home. Verena's father was a nuclear physicist at Chalk River. "He was a great dad," she says, "but had reservations about hiring women. The women's movement wasn't fully fledged yet. 'They'll have babies and leave the job,' he'd say. But for me, there were no limits. I have an older brother, but Dad treated us the same. I learned soldering, how to cut things, electronics, building a telescope. It helped me be bloody-minded about what I wanted to study."

Her passion for marine biology never wavered and she's earned impressive credentials. An undergraduate science degree from McMaster University was followed by a master's and a doctorate from Yale. She's a fellow of the prestigious Royal Society of Canada, and she won the Steacie Foundation Prize, an award granted to only one Canadian scientist each year. While on this intense career track, she married John Garrett, a marine policy consultant, and became mother to Arielle, now 12.

All her work has concentrated on marine life, but that lifelong interest has had many guises. Her undergraduate work began with a study of the relationship of animals and sediment in the vast tidal flats of the Bay of Fundy in Nova Scotia, or as she puts it in the vernacular, "studying clams and mud." In graduate school, she incorporated aspects of structural engineering and fluid mechanics into a study on how stony coral reefs in Jamaica survive during storm surges. That work became the basis for re-establishing some of those reefs after Hurricane Allen destroyed them.

Jobs were scarce for marine biologists when she graduated — even for those with impressive doctorates — so in 1980 she accepted a post-doctoral fellowship to study worms at the Institute of Ocean Sciences near Sidney. But one day, Verena took a walk around the grounds, a walk that refocussed the course of her career and her life. "I wandered into one of the sheds and noticed Pisces IV, a submersible," she recalls. Intrigued, she asked "one of the guys" to take her for a dive. The request was granted. "I fell in love with the submersible after I began looking at the animals living on the walls of Saanich Inlet," says the slim professor.

Captivated by the astonishing life forms in Saanich Inlet, Verena turned the submersible into a tool for studying inaccessible colonies of fauna because, she says, "it's the only way to uncover what lives on the steep, deep fjord walls." Subsequently, she has made more than 130 piloted dives in B.C.'s fjords, especially Jervis Inlet. She investigated animal societies in their undersea environment, studied glass sponges and corals and tested ecological theories on community diversity. She published her findings in the prestigious journal *Nature*. The University of Victoria took note and offered her a professorship in biology and earth and ocean sciences.

Her know-how with submersibles led to a further evolution in her marine research: over the last decade she's become renowned for her expertise on the animals that survive at hydrothermal (hot) vents as deep as three miles below the ocean surface in temperatures that can exceed 750°F.

In her university office, its walls festooned with colour photos of hot-vent animals, Verena takes one of her scarce free hours to explain that hydrothermal vents are created along mid-ocean ridges where new material rises between the spreading tectonic plates that make up the earth's outer crust. As the ocean floor rifts slowly along the underwater volcanic mountain ranges girdling the globe, cold water sinks into the fissures and is superheated by the rocks below. The heat boosts the water's buoyancy so it rises through the vents. "The escaping plumes are not just ordinary seawater," says Verena. "The mineral particles suspended in these streams are deposited around the fissures and build up oddly shaped chimneys that resemble the helter-skelter construction of coral reefs. I brought back one of those chimneys. It's now at the Institute of Ocean Sciences in Sidney."

Hot vents were discovered in 1977 off the Galápagos Islands when a group of scientists sent a submersible down to look for evidence of how the sea floor spreads. They found a bonus: proof that a heat source underlying the spreading ridges thrusts scalding water plumes through the ocean floor.

"What so surprised biologists," continues Verena, "is that during its journey through the earth's magma, the water becomes laced with hydrogen sulphide, a chemical poisonous to life as we know it. We might expect the vents' surroundings to be empty of living creatures, but large groups of worms — we call them 'vestimentiferans' — molluscs and arthropods thrive in that hot, dark sea." The Galápagos discovery spawned further finds of spreading ridges around the world, including the Juan de Fuca Ridge off Vancouver Island, Washington and Oregon. Biologists have now discovered more than 500 new animal species at various ridges.

Before encountering hot-vent fauna, scientists believed that all animals on the planet survive directly or indirectly through the solar energy trapped by green plants and converted into nutrients through photosynthesis: animals eat plants or eat animals that have eaten plants. But in the sunless reaches where hot springs spout, photosynthesis has been replaced by chemosynthesis. In the perpetual dark, primitive bacteria that may have a two- to three-billion-year history have learned to transform energy-rich hydrogen sulphide into nutrients that nourish other species. These bacteria either live inside some of the hot-vent animals and supply energy directly to their hosts, or they float around and are ingested by other, larger, species.

"Tubeworms are good examples," Verena elaborates. "They have no mouths, guts or anuses. Just a giant sausage in a tube with a red tuft sticking out the top. That sausage turns out to be a highly evolved adaptation to vents: it is filled with red blood and bacteria. Why bother slurping up bacteria for food when you can just grow them inside you? The worms pick up oxygen, dissolved sulphide and carbon dioxide with their gills. These compounds travel in the blood to the bacteria, which use energy from the oxidation of sulphide to fix the carbon dioxide into scrumptious sugars. The sugars pass to the worm — very efficient!"

What interests Verena particularly is how these animals differ from "normal" animals. "Their habitat is so extreme," she continues. "These palm worms, limpets, clams, they all have primitive characteristics." She notes the fauna are ancient and have managed to survive in part because there has been no competition at the locations where they live. Yet they've evolved to live at the edge, forever under threat of death from sudden volcanic action. They offer lines of genetic diversity not found elsewhere, giving us a glimpse of antiquity. Hot-vent animals show us that life on earth is even more diverse than we had supposed and that animals can evolve to find energy in chemicals once thought to be fatal. These animals are "living fossils." It's now the prevalent theory that hot-vent bacteria may have pre-existed, and be the ancestors of, all other life forms.

To continue these fascinating studies after submersibles supplied by other nations were no longer available, Verena became a member of the Canadian Scientific Submersible Facility, which raised funds for and now operates ROPOS, a submarine activated by remote control down to depths of three miles. With this craft, Verena and her colleagues can illuminate and photograph deep-sea structures and organisms, recover equipment, perform geological and biological sampling and conduct surveys.

One worrisome aspect of hot-vent research is the threat of ecological destruction of the deep-water sites. The scientific community is attempting to be non-intrusive, but at the spreading ridges off Papua New Guinea, mining companies are digging for gold deposits bubbling up around the vents, with little concern for preserving the site. "We need international, binding agreements to keep these unique places from being destroyed," Verena says fervently. Fortunately, the Juan de Fuca Ridge hot-vent area has recently been designated as a "pilot marine protected area" by the federal government.

Her enthusiasm for the life and characteristics of the deeper recesses of the world's salt water continues, leaving little time for her to cruise on the family's 24-foot Sea Ray. "I'm in mid-career now," she says with characteristic self-deprecation and a wry grin. "So now I'm learning new skills in dealing with people." She's describing the slippery politics of negotiating two projects that require substantial government funding — from federal, provincial and state governments in both Canada and the U.S. She's part of a team trying to create "Neptune," a $250-million project that aims to build a network of unstaffed seafloor observatories around the Juan de Fuca Ridge.

"We've had major volcanic episodes at the ridge over the past five years," says Verena, "but we didn't know much about them until our submersible's cameras revealed big new lava beds on the ocean floor." She adds that providing power to the instruments at the ridge is difficult now because batteries deplete quickly, but Neptune will establish observatories that are linked to shore by submarine cable carrying fibre-optic communications. Once installed, Neptune will contribute to the understanding of earthquake hazards, the impacts of climate change on fisheries and gas hydrates along the continental margins. Canada's Hertzberg Institute will be responsible for managing the huge amounts of data to be collected.

Verena is also working with a group of other marine scientists to establish a scaled-down British Columbia version of Neptune called VENUS (Victoria Experimental Network UnderSea). Again, the project uses fibre-optic cables and provides a completely new technique for observing the sea. "Neptune is the father of VENUS," she says, "but VENUS is a test bed allowing us to build a database and develop ways to do the science." B.C. is a prime candidate for such studies because of its wide range of marine environments, valuable fish stocks, sensitive habitats, marine mammals, active shipping and urban growth.

The fibre-optic cables will be laid from three land sites. The first, extending from Tsawwassen into the Strait of Georgia, will monitor Fraser delta stability at the ferry and container ports, and will measure water circulation and fish migration. The second cable, stretching across the entrance of Saanich Inlet, will study anoxic renewal and how microbes respond. The third, reaching into Juan de Fuca Strait from Vancouver Island beyond Race Rocks, will study how offshore events influence the coast. The cables will deliver power for instruments, lights and robots. "For the first time," says Verena, "we won't have to wait for data from recovered instruments — it'll be delivered immediately as events in the ocean unfold."

Why is such instrumentation useful? "We don't have much knowledge of the movement of currents in either Juan de Fuca Strait or the Strait of Georgia. What is the estuarine circulation of the Fraser River? Knowing about circulation allows us to develop plans to contain oil spills and direct search-and-rescue." Further project goals include examining the effects of climate change and tracking salmon by attaching tiny acoustic tags to hatchery fish and monitoring them through high-frequency receivers. Each fish will have an individual identifier. "We'll be able to understand salmon survival, juvenile behaviour, their comings and goings, and how water characteristics and the presence of zooplankton influence the whole ecological chain, including whales." For example, hydrophones can continuously monitor killer and grey whales and even see how boat traffic affects their movements. She adds that scientists will be able to devise all kinds of new experiments since data collection is no longer intermittent and will be connected directly to computer banks.

What Verena is ardent about in this project is the amount of data that will make "good science." "We have no good long-term ocean data sets," she says. "Much of what we rely on to make decisions is guesswork. With these two projects we'll have a capacity to truly monitor seismic events, water column characteristics, the effects of El Niño and fish movements. And all of it should be available to be mined by bright minds everywhere."

In the meantime, besides writing proposals and scientific papers, Verena still gets out to sea. The offshore trips on research vessels to further decipher deep-ocean secrets energize and motivate her. "The sea is an alien world with a wonderful set of adaptations," she says. "You can't see inside it — it's a mystery. The sea presents a wonderful intellectual and spiritual challenge. The sea is my life."

Frank Brown
rock solid

Heiltsuk tribal member Frank Brown is taking a whack at the ballooning unemployment plaguing Bella Bella, an ancient fishing village on Campbell Island on B.C.'s central coast. The 38-year-old entrepreneur gazes at McLoughlin Bay, with its long, slender dock peppered with anti-slip roofing shingles, and points to two traditional "Glwa" (ocean-going) canoes, their bows painted and proud. The canoes are part of See Quest, the unique eco-tourism business Frank and his wife, Kathy ("my partner in life and business"), founded six years ago. A young employee is scrubbing out a canoe as we walk toward the vessels with their vivid red, black and green seawolf, raven and other clan crest motifs. I notice the sculpted hulls are fibreglass. "Fibreglass, not cedar?" I ask. "Certainly," Frank replies. "They're fibreglass with Kevlar. The material is much better for novice canoers, it can take a pounding, it's easy to maintain and it doesn't crack. It's wise to adapt modern materials to traditional methods of transportation."

See Quest introduces people to Heiltsuk culture and uses its traditions to create a modern business in a region called the "gateway to the Great Bear Rainforest," but which is hurting from the decline in fishing and logging. When BC Ferries' "Discovery Coast" *Queen of Chilliwack* stops in Bella Bella (on its summer runs from Port Hardy to Prince Rupert), See Quest's canoes spring into action. Frank takes interested passengers on a paddle to nearby Shearwater, another small settlement, stopping to show them an old memorial pole — an eagle chief with cedar hat — peeking out from the forest on a burial island. Along the way, he explains that the name "Bella Bella" is a Hudson's Bay Company adaptation of the tribal name *Bil-Billa*. From 1833 to 1843, the HBC ran Fort McLoughlin here, one of its earliest western trading posts.

Frank's tour also includes guided walks and visits to the Heiltsuk interpretive centre — a mini-longhouse — with its posters explaining the eulachon fish-oil trade of the past. Flocks of painted paddles decorate the walls. Crushed white, purple and lavender urchin shells, their innards processed next door at the Native Fish Plant for Japanese sushi chefs, define the paths around the mini-longhouse. Frank plans to construct a full-scale longhouse, the first to be built on the coast in 150 years, for use by both the community and tourists. After a short walk over a trail flanked by thimbleberries, he shows me four brightly painted house poles carved by elder Stanley George, ready to grace the façade when construction is completed.

After the tour, visitors are invited to eat coho salmon roasted on cedar sticks over an open fire. Seated on rough wooden chairs next to the firepit, in an area loosely covered with blue tarps sagging with puddles from the most recent downpour in this rain forest, Frank tells me his hopes to expand See Quest. While we wait for the ferry to disgorge its passengers, Frank jumps up and circles the fire, tucking in new logs and rotating the salmon his visitors will feast on later.

Frank sees himself as a modern man transformed by traditional methods. There's a stillness about his tall frame, as if he's gathered himself in and feels solid to the core. Now widely respected as a community leader, this father of four ran afoul of the law in his early teens. Frank reveals that as a small lad he used to cry to go fishing with his dad, a salmon gillnetter, even though he suffered from seasickness. When Frank was only eight, his father died in an accident involving alcohol. His mother did her best to keep the family of six children together and moved to the Lower Mainland to earn her teaching certificate. Frank spent three years in Chilliwack but loathed the place, finding it too confining. "I was born to be free on the water, on the beach and the forests. Inland, I felt trapped." After Frank turned 11, his mother moved the family back to Bella Bella, where she taught pre-school for many years. Although happy to be back in his childhood playground, Frank felt the loss of his father deeply and, over time, his grief became stained with anger. He acted out; he skipped school; he committed several break-and-enters.

Then he led a group of older boys on a break-in to steal alcohol from a local bootlegger, and the petty theft escalated into a serious assault. Normally, this type of crime would have put him away in a juvenile detention centre, one of hundreds of youths learning crime and attitude from other mutinous kids. As he says, "Just another Indian gone bad, another statistic." But community elders — especially his uncle, Robert Hall — interceded with Provincial Court Justice Cunliffe Barnett and asked that Frank be subjected instead to a traditional Heiltsuk sentence: banishment. The judge agreed, and at the age of 14, Frank was exiled for eight months to Chatfield Island. Except for occasional visits from relatives bringing food, he was alone.

The banishment reshaped the young man. "My body was polluted with alcohol and my spirit was sick," he recalls in a documentary made a decade later. "I kept saying to myself, 'I don't care, I don't care about anything.' That's why I was dangerous. I was on my way to becoming a hard-core juvie, heading straight downhill." In the film, Frank acts out his experience. Wearing a dark, menacing mask, he runs in the woods, full of anger and resentment. Then one evening, he sees an ugly, dwarf-like being among the trees. "It was hooting and laughing at me. I was afraid and said a prayer for help and strength. When I dared walk toward it, it shrank away. There was nothing there. It was me, my imagination. A manifestation of my dark side." In the re-enactment, Frank's mask opens and a second mask is visible: its colours are a happy red and blue.

His life-altering banishment completed, Frank returned to Bella Bella. "The experience made me think," he says. "I recognized that if you're not responsible for yourself, others will be glad to do it for you. I was determined to take charge of myself. I paid my debt and had a new lease on life. I wanted to redeem myself in the eyes of my community." Fortunately, he lived in the right place to follow one of his passions: the ocean. Boating, fishing or walking streams with his grandfather to count salmon, his need to be on the water never waned. One summer, he signed on as deck hand on the *Thomas Crosby*, a United Church marine mission bringing God to villages, logging camps and lighthouses between Port Hardy and Alaska. "I loved it," he says. "I saw many villages. Got a coast-wide perspective." His interest in learning also grew. He spent a week at the B.C. Youth Parliament in Victoria. "That was a really different experience," he says. "I learned how government works, parliamentary procedure, and about people and politics and ambition." After finishing high school, he attended tourism and outdoor-recreation courses at the Vancouver Native Education Centre and completed a small-business incubator program at the British Columbia Institute of Technology. He met Kathy, a Nuu-chah-nulth woman from Vancouver Island's west coast, and they married. But he returned to the central coast because, he says, "When I'm on the water I'm communing with the Creator; it's like a spirit — beautiful and serene yet powerful and scary."

The plans for Vancouver's Expo in 1986, with its themes of transportation and communications, further energized the young Heiltsuk. Musing upon the traditional canoe, he recognized that this vehicle embodied both Expo themes. He decided canoes could become more than museum pieces; he vowed to re-create history and worked with village carvers to fashion the ancient shape from an eight-ton red-cedar log. "It was a learning thing," explains Frank. "It took time, but the whole community got involved." The canoe carried Frank and 12 other paddlers from Bella Bella to Expo. Accompanied by herring skiffs and gillnetters, the team camped on beaches during the 22-day odyssey south. The voyage moved Frank deeply and made him feel as if he'd paddled back in time. "We had a chance to see the land through the eyes of our ancestors. After paddling some hours, we'd go ashore on the old canoe skids and say to ourselves, 'Wow, the old people were here before us.'"

The trip also fired the imagination of many coastal tribes and revived memories of their heritage in marine transportation. A "Paddle to Seattle" followed three years later (partially funded by T-shirt sales) and then, after Frank issued a challenge to other coastal tribes, Bella Bella hosted a *qa'tu'was*, "people gathering together," with 23 great canoes from Washington and British Columbia participating in the festival. The success of this revival triggered the plan for See Quest.

While Frank is committed to eco-tourism and resource conservation, he earns his main livelihood from the herring spawn on kelp fishery. "A sustainable fishery," he emphasizes. "It's a non-kill operation. Herring can spawn up to six times a year; basically, we collect the 'overspawn.'" The Heiltsuk tribe, which, he says proudly, won its traditional rights to harvest herring spawn through the courts, usually fishes only 10 days a year. It is now the largest B.C. producer of this delicacy, selling most of the harvest to the Japanese, who call the gold-coloured eggs *kuzonuko kombu*. Before the short fishing season begins, Frank and other fishermen collect *Macrocystis* (giant kelp) stalks and fronds and suspend them from floats in places herring are likely to spawn. Once the kelp leaves are encrusted with a quarter inch of the crunchy caviar, they're gathered, trimmed, brined and packaged at the Bella Bella Native Fish Plant. Last year, Heiltsuk licence holders harvested 109,000 kilograms which fetched well over $3.5 million. Characteristically, Frank runs the Spawn on Kelp Committee.

Will aboriginal eco-tourism on the central B.C. coast replace the livelihood gained from fishing? Frank sees the potential of eco-tourism but will undoubtedly continue to combine careers. "This is part of our traditional fishing grounds and the old sea highway," he explains. "It's been a gathering place for centuries. But it's also uncrowded, pristine, with clear waters, clean air and primeval forests — an environment no longer available to westerners. It has a temperate climate and is accessible. There's nothing like it anywhere."

Frank's life is consumed by living his heritage and combining it with sustainable development. "We have a lot to offer," he says, abandoning the sometimes-ponderous speech patterns of a future elder. His tone catches fire. "Cultural diversity, time-honoured knowledge — that's why I'm in this business. I value our traditions and want to share them. I could just host sport fishermen, but I want more. I don't want to liquidate the inheritance of our kids. In our legends, we talk seven generations ahead.

"It's challenging to live here," he continues. "I live in a cross-cultural environment and thus have a chance to engage in a somewhat traditional lifestyle. I love the ocean and its vessels. The sea can be beautiful and serene, or powerful and scary. You can't say the sea is good or bad. It's what it is. When it gets blustery, you have to have faith, stay the course, weather the storm. You must prepare for life the same way. That's why I have respect for the sea. The old people say between the sky and the land lies the sea, a sacred place. You must be respectful and careful because the sea is full of uncertainty. It's a lesson we can share as First Nations. Because in our world, we're all in this canoe together."

Paul Spong
the eavesdropper

Paul Spong's OrcaLab roosts on a small bight on Hanson Island, a fair-sized chunk of rock east of Malcolm Island in Johnstone Strait, the passage that separates Vancouver Island from B.C.'s mainland. Summers, when the orcas migrate, it's a hub filled with people learning about these mammals, the world's largest dolphins. The creatures' highly developed brains — the second largest of any animal, nearly four times the mass of the human brain — and their deep sense of family connection are just two of the characteristics that attracted Paul Spong to study them in the wild.

When I arrive at Hanson Island by water taxi (besides Paul, his wife and research partner Helen Symonds, and daughter Anna, no one inhabits the island), Paul is out on a short foray into the strait to monitor an orca pod. While awaiting his return, I wander from the couple's log-and-plank house down the boardwalk to a silvery grey wood building perched over the water. It's the nerve centre of OrcaLab, where listeners, using an array of black-faced receivers and a manual switchboard, track the orcas' migration through the nearby narrows. Boxes filled with audiotapes of recorded orca conversations line the walls. Several loudspeakers dangle from the walls and emit an occasional staticky bleep, interspersed with the high-pitched squeals and whistles of chatting orcas. The speakers are connected to a network of six remote hydrophone stations, a quiet, unobtrusive way to eavesdrop on the northern resident community of orcas that travel and feed here in the summer. The goal? To "research orcas without interference and to follow the lives of the individuals and families that make up their communities."

I meet student workers from England, Austria and Vancouver who staff the lab and camp out in sleeping bags in a small loft. They're resting on this sun-drenched day because they stayed up most of the night to monitor the various voyaging orca clans. The young people are also tracking the reintegration of Springer — the orphaned orca whose heart-rending loneliness garnered worldwide attention — into her family.

After Paul pulls up to the rocks in his fast aluminum skiff, we talk outside, seated on old-fashioned wooden deck chairs. In his soft New Zealand accent, tempered by decades of living in North America, the scientist tells me that after being born in 1939 in Auckland, he grew up in Whakatane on the Bay of Plenty. He did the usual sailing, fishing and swimming of a kid living near the ocean, but although the ocean breakers crashed on the beaches where he played, his love of salt water only solidified when he became mesmerized by the black-and-white mammals that dwell in it. After completing undergraduate work in New Zealand, he chose the University of California at Los Angeles to study physiological psychology. "UCLA research was building a bridge between the emerging areas of brain science and behavioural science. It was a wonderful opportunity to participate in the beginnings of modern neuroscience. I was fascinated by the brain and by brain functions." After Paul earned his PhD in 1966, he took a half-time neurophysiological research position at the University of British Columbia, and another in behavioural research at the Vancouver Aquarium, home to a newly captured orca called Skana. The latter job permanently changed the set of his sails.

"The Vancouver Aquarium was the first institution that really displayed orcas," continues Paul, a slight man who speaks with intensity but with care not to overstate. He spent a couple of years studying the orca and topics like the animal's visual learning. But he soon recognized Skana was an acoustic animal and grew uncomfortable about the way she was housed, isolated from her kin and deprived of her natural sensory environment. "We knew little about orcas — just that they're social animals living in groups — but it was quite obvious that Skana's was a highly developed mind. I felt it simply inappropriate to keep her in a small concrete pen."

In 1969, Paul travelled to Alert Bay to learn about orcas living in the wild. Within a year he'd founded OrcaLab and established the first base camp on Hanson Island's Blackney Pass, the location he still inhabits today. For the next decade he spent summers observing the cetaceans, but in 1979, after marrying Helen Symonds and giving up his work at UBC, he made the research station into a year-round facility and the study of orcas his life and livelihood. They raised their daughter, Anna, here and consider her not only a family member but also "a most valuable employee." Anna designs and maintains the websites, including the www.orca-live.net/, which transmits live webcasts.

Over the past 30 years, OrcaLab's researchers have discovered many previously unknown aspects of orca life by listening through the hydrophone network that now covers roughly 20 square miles. In British Columbia and Washington, the 200-member northern resident community and a southern resident community of about 80 orcas occupy fairly defined territories. Additional transient groups also journey in these waters.

Orcas live in matrilineal, closely bonded family groups made up of a mother and her progeny. Several families together form a clan. The families and their members have each been identified by their markings and voices, allowing researchers to track their numbers and migration patterns. Each group has its own dialect. But it is unlikely that we will be able to understand the meaning of their communications. "We can make some guesses about their activities," explains Paul, his brown eyes often sweeping the strait in front of us. "We know when the whales are resting, when they're excited or hunting. But as to the content of their exchanges, I don't really anticipate any breakthroughs. They aren't likely to swim up to you and start a conversation."

To fund OrcaLab and continue the research, Paul established the non-profit Pacific Orca Society. An English group, the Born

Free Foundation, provides core funding of about $24,000 a year, while other organizations and people interested in whale research donate as well, giving the society a total annual income of roughly $100,000. Paul views that amount as adequate. "Perhaps it's not much to perform our rather complicated research, but I'm satisfied we're doing enough and have enough. We're always happy when people want to come and help us. I don't spend much time actively looking for money."

Having studied orcas, Paul is convinced they have much to teach us. He's observed the orcas' group-based, intensely social life. He tells me the division of resident and transient orca clans goes back 100,000 years, and that these animals have thus achieved a way of life enabling them to flourish over the long term. Among themselves, they live in a non-violent, co-operative society. Paul believes we humans live co-operatively too, but have a dark side that can ultimately destroy us. "Because we're such different animals, it's hard to know if we can evolve like the orcas. But I find it interesting and encouraging to think that a big-brained, social animal has achieved a lifestyle that has allowed it to succeed over eons. Whether we are capable of a similar kind of transition, I don't know."

He also contends that whales are the world's environmental barometer, and if they are extinguished, humanity may well follow. "I certainly believe we have endangered orca populations. In our region the numbers have declined for seven straight years. The loss of females in their prime years is especially troubling." He cites water and acoustic pollution, loss of habitat and loss of food supply. Industrial developments in urban areas like Vancouver and Seattle are a major source of pollutants. Orcas live on top of the food chain and thus accumulate every pollutant absorbed by the lower orders. Other toxins are carried on ocean currents across long distances. "Even when we clean up our own waters, global pollution affects whales here. So if the whales die … "

In addition, Paul is deeply concerned about the renewal of commercial whaling. He worked hard with Greenpeace in the 1970s in the quest to save the whales, but became less active after the

International Whaling Commission (IWC) agreed to a moratorium on commercial whaling in 1982. "I thought the issue had been settled," he sighs. "And now there may be spill-over from aboriginal hunts into commercial whaling." Paul would like to see the killing of whales by humans stopped completely, although he admits it's not a simple issue.

"With aboriginal whaling, you're confronted with the nutritional need of people. It's tough to oppose people's need to survive, even when dealing with an endangered species like the bowhead whale." He cites starving people like the Chukota in Siberia and concedes it's difficult to tell them they shouldn't kill whales. But, he says, the Japanese aren't starving so why are they hunting whales? He absolutely opposes the "scientific whaling" the Japanese claim to conduct. He declares the Japanese rationalization — learning about whales, what they eat, or their reproductive state by killing them — is antiquated science and that the Japanese body of scientific literature is very thin indeed. "Our non-lethal methods for studying whales are absolutely superior."

Paul sits almost motionless, woolly lamb's ears fluttering in a small garden plot behind his head. He speaks softly, voice low, but there's no missing his anger when we discuss a "cultural rationale" for the killing of whales — the justification used by the Washington Makah. "The rationale the Makah use is something created to bypass those arguing that aboriginal whaling should only be allowed for nutritional reasons. The Makah aren't hungry." He adds that the IWC has rejected "traditional practices" as a reason for renewing whaling, but that the Makah have created "spillover problems." The practice has hamstrung the U.S., he says, because they cannot on the one hand allow the Makah to kill whales for cultural reasons, and then refuse the Japanese, who use the same rationale.

Paul sees the Makah whale hunt as a "brilliant" device to create problems in international whale management. He stresses that the Makah would be better served by finding more direct methods to solve their problems of unemployment and pride. "The Makah have been led down the garden path by people with a completely different agenda, people uninterested in the welfare of the Makah nation. Instead, they're interested in creating disarray within the IWC to allow commercial whaling to resume. The Makah are being used as pawns in somebody else's game — a cynical game."

Paul points out that commercial whaling lacks economic credibility. "We get much more benefit from live whales than from simply treating them as a protein resource. Even the economic benefits from whale watching are far superior to killing whales." He argues that the total number of whales worldwide is still depressed, that habitat and climate changes are making the future of whales uncertain, and that, consequently, we should do everything in our power to preserve them. "To start commercial whaling for some sort of petty reason doesn't make any sense at all."

Captive orcas also worry Paul. For years he's campaigned to free Corky, an orca belonging to the northern resident community A5 pod, captured in 1969 and part of the "orca entertainment industry" at the San Diego Sea World. Another orca, Lolita, a former member of the southern resident community, has performed at the Miami Seaquarium since 1971. Paul would like to see both caged females return to the wild. "Look," he says, "when we began studying these animals 30 years ago, we knew little about them. But we've learned that orcas can reintegrate into their families, just like the baby whale, Springer." He's convinced the two captive orcas may still have the potential to rejoin with their families, as they're relatively young in orca terms (many females live 80 years). "We would benefit from the knowledge gained and potentially benefit the families they come from. The experience with Springer looks great so far, but we don't understand the long-term effects of reintegration."

Soon, the summer bustle at OrcaLab will dwindle. By December, the orcas usually move on to their winter feeding grounds — no one knows exactly where. Visitors and students depart, leaving Paul and Helen (and sometimes Anna) behind to contend with months of rain and blustery weather. In anticipation, the peeled silver and orange logs colonizing the rocky beach are tied down with yellow floating line, ready to sacrifice themselves to warmth and cooking fires when 50-knot, southeasterly storms batter the region. Alone, says Paul, but not lonely. The pair is busy working on orca conservation issues, writing articles, attending meetings on whaling, doing the books.

Paul is content.

After more than two decades living on an island only inhabited by his family, he describes his life on the water as "splendid." "It's a wonderful thing to have this opportunity to study orcas, to live here and work with those I love. I feel privileged in having an endlessly fascinating, interesting and entertaining subject for my work. Every day brings new experiences, thoughts, ideas and challenges. I feel extraordinarily fortunate to be where I am, doing what I am doing."

Charlie White
the evangelist of fishing

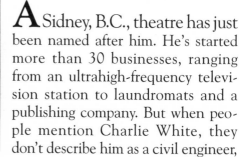

A Sidney, B.C., theatre has just been named after him. He's started more than 30 businesses, ranging from an ultrahigh-frequency television station to laundromats and a publishing company. But when people mention Charlie White, they don't describe him as a civil engineer, entrepreneur or philanthropist. Only one association jumps up like a frisky salmon out of the water: fishing. Charlie White — his name is almost a trademark — is known around the world for his knowledge about fish: their habitat, habits, characteristics, behaviour and, of course, how to catch them. People have called him a fishing guru; his fishing prowess is legendary. Many of his business interests have been related to fishing, like the invention of his downrigger or, more recently, his virtual fishing machine, which gives anglers a chance to catch the big one without being on the water.

The day I meet Charlie in his home's sunroom on Vancouver Island's Saanich Inlet, where he lives with his wife, Darlene, he's already spent three hours fishing on the Bayliner Trophy now moored at the dock below. He caught only a few small salmon and tossed them back, but he's happy. What counts is the freedom to fish, engage the downrigger, hook the silvery creatures, be out on the water, smell the salt air.

During his long life, Charlie has developed some deceptively simple principles to live by. "I've always believed you must live where you enjoy yourself," says the slim 75-year-old, "because life is not a dress rehearsal." Charlie has followed that philosophy. Born in Pittsburgh, Pennsylvania, far from the sea, he earned a scholarship to Cornell University after winning a statewide "Quiz Kids" competition. He majored in civil engineering at this Ivy League school, and after serving in the navy during World War II, he joined a firm specializing in water and sewage treatment. One day he realized he just didn't want to spend his life being known as a sewage sludge expert, so he switched to the Aluminum Company of America (Alcoa), a huge firm working to transform its product lines from warplane raw material into consumer goods. Charlie found it exciting to help design and market such innovations as aluminum pistons for General Motors cars, but life in Pittsburgh had its drawbacks.

Charlie had loved fishing since he was five, but the nearby rivers and streams were polluted, so he moved to Oregon to join that state's Fish Commission as a biologist and filmmaker. From there, he became involved with building the first ultra-high-frequency television station in Portland. He also met and married his first wife, Anne. The couple opted for a honeymoon in Victoria, where, of course, Charlie went fishing. "I just fell in love with the place and thought it was absolutely beautiful. Before catching the ferry to Port Angeles, I looked up television and radio stations in the phone book (there was no television station in Victoria then) and noted there was a downtown radio station, so I walked in and asked to see the manager." When the owner, Dave Armstrong, came out, he exclaimed, "Oh my god, it's Charlie White." It turned out he'd read about Charlie and the Portland UHF station in the latest copy of *Broadcasting Magazine*. Charlie told him he'd like to build such a station in Canada; he and his wife missed their ferry. By 1956, Armstrong and Charlie had applied for a broadcasting licence, and Charlie moved to Victoria permanently. "When anyone asks about immigrating here, I always say I was a Canadian born on the wrong side of the border," he quips. "But I could see all this wonderful, protected fishing water around here and in Portland there was only river or open-ocean fishing. I got seasick on the ocean and here was this nice calm water ... "

Charlie co-founded Victoria's CHEK-TV, but some time later accepted a buyout offer from a Vancouver station. Opportunities to manage the biggest television stations in Seattle and Miami materialized at once. Charlie turned them down. Instead, he became a fishing guide. "After I sold my portion of CHEK-TV, I just went fishing all the time and got to be a pretty good fisherman. I owned a little 25-foot cabin cruiser and had the rods and reels (don't call them 'fishing poles,' a pole is something you put telephone lines on). People began paying me to take them fishing. There were other fishing guides, but they stayed in Saanich Inlet and used deep tackle and heavy lines. I fished with light tackle — more of a sporting approach to fishing — in the Gulf Islands."

By the late 1950s, he'd established a reputation as a guide and kept his boat on a mooring buoy outside his house on Saanich Inlet. He picked up his customers at Swartz Bay, now well known as a terminal from which ferries transport millions of passengers and cars between Vancouver Island, the Gulf Islands and mainland B.C., but then an isolated backwater. His customers boarded from the bay's tiny dock; Charlie took the early birds fishing from 5:00 A.M. until noon, then took his second group until evening. He'd clean the fish, run home, siphon gas from the big drums in his yard and refill the boat's tanks. He remembers the long hours and the fatigue during the summer months. To become known as a fishing guide — and to justify the high prices he charged: $10 for the first hour and $6 an hour thereafter, including the boat, lures and tackle — he applied the personal touch. First, he took the "head guy at the tourist bureau" fishing. "I caught him a lot of fish and he was so impressed he sent me tons of clients." He then invited the Empress Hotel's manager to go fishing. On that day "we just loaded the boat with fish and he was so impressed he sent people like Bob Hope and all kinds of executive parties, so I had a lot of business."

Charlie loved guiding but reveals that, financially, it was a disaster. He cites the expenses to run the boat, and the floating debris that repeatedly whacked the propeller, requiring replacements costing several hundred dollars each. "At the end of the season, with gas, bait and repairs, I actually lost money," he recalls, playing with his reading glasses. He was also surprised that the pressure of being a fishing guide exceeded that of working as a young hotshot engineer at Alcoa. "Just to give an example, one day this company president and two vice-presidents flew in from Denver in a private plane. They'd heard stories about me. They're fidgety, drumming their fingers on the side of their chairs, and I could just hear them thinking, 'Well, Mr. Expert, where are the fish?' Well, some days the fish aren't there and they won't bite no matter what you do. I found it highly stressful."

His next venture was quite a switch: coin-operated laundromats. He teamed up with Art Phillips, who later served as Vancouver's mayor. Knowing that profitability can quickly erode when the washing machines break down, Charlie wrote one of his fishing clients, the president of Maytag, whose foreign sales manager was assigned to work with Charlie on a coin-laundry franchise. Charlie still chuckles at the recollection. "The manager thought the Maytag president had completely lost his marbles, asking him to negotiate with a fishing guide, so he wrote me a polite letter explaining that this was a business requiring an office and everything." Charlie responded by sending in his résumé, giving the manager such a shock he flew to Victoria and concluded the deal in person.

Over the years, Charlie founded many businesses. He likes to create and build an enterprise, but then, he explains, someone always comes along wanting to buy it. While the laundromats were being established across western Canada, he co-founded CFAX Radio (again with Art Phillips as partner), still a staple station on Vancouver Island. He also participated in local affairs, serving on committees to bring more tourists to Victoria. Convinced that everyone likes fish, Charlie conceived of the idea of "an aquarium in reverse," a marine-life exhibit that puts people in the tank while the fish freely swim outside, although confined by a fence. This concept grew into the Undersea Gardens, still one of the most popular attractions in Victoria. Charlie holds the patents for this novel idea and built three more undersea gardens in the United States. His personal life also evolved. He and Anne had three sons, but divorced in 1980. Eight years later, he married Darlene, a gardening writer.

Although Charlie quit being a full-time fishing guide, his love of fishing never waned. In the early 1970s, a local newspaper editor asked him to write a story on how to catch crabs. As Charlie had spent years telling people about fishing of all kinds, he thought it would be fun to try his hand at writing about it. "So I sat down and wrote a little *Sunday Magazine* story about catching crabs, and I couldn't believe the people who called me saying how much they enjoyed it. So I decided it could be a little book and dictated it in a couple of hours." He asked cartoonist Nelson Dewey to illustrate the booklet, then visited a local printer and ordered 5,000 copies. The printer discouraged Charlie, saying that he'd be lucky to sell 500. "This was 1969 and the guy was shaking his head. 'And you want to sell it for a dollar?' he kept asking me. Well, we printed them, they sold out in a year and that tome has sold 100,000 copies." (It's still in print and now retails for $8.95.)

With that success, Charlie, realizing he really knew much more about salmon fishing than crabbing, composed his next opus, *How to Catch Salmon — Basic Techniques*, which still sells today. One book followed another, with such titles as *How to Catch Trout, Living off the Sea, How to Catch Shellfish, 105 Fishing Secrets* and *Quick Tips for Catching Halibut*, and soon, of course, Charlie started the aptly named Saltaire Publishing, through which he published his own books and those by other authors as well. Typically, he sold the company and his books are now published by Heritage House. He also taught courses and seminars on sport fishing, covering such topics as lures, getting them to the proper depth, knowing when and where to go for good fishing, how to read water and the best season for catching different fish.

More inventions appeared on Charlie's agenda. Because he seems to thrive on multitasking, nothing has been a full-time occupation for him, and one day, when he got tired of waiting for the charcoal to heat up in his barbeque, he dreamed up Son of Hibachi, a fast, tabletop, self-cleaning unit that has sold millions. He also noted that new fishing techniques with nylon nets and fish finders were "cleaning out the surface fish and strip mining the ocean. The only fish able to spawn were those that swam deep under the nets, so we had to go deeper and deeper to catch fish. I hated it because you had to put heavy weights on your lines and there's no sport in dragging around this five-pound piece of lead." Charlie decided there had to be a better way, so to get a lure deep enough, he put down a second line that would pop free when a fish struck. He experimented with a window-sash weight, clothesline and clothespin, tied it to a cleat on his boat's stern and found that the jury-rig worked. He then built a model out of a two-by-four with a pulley and a wire, and remembers his glee that this functioned even better: "I thought, 'Hell, this is great.' I took some other people along and they said, 'Holy cow, this is wonderful.'" He took his idea to Blayney Scott of Scotty Fishing, Marine and Outdoor Products and together they designed the Scotty downrigger. Scott Plastics developed the manufacturing process and made the moulds, and the downriggers, now in various designs, some electrically driven, sell around the world. Charlie collected royalties for a number of years. He also lays claim to having invented the Thinking Man's Sinker and the first artificial ice packs made of plastic.

The books, inventions and courses made his name well known in the boating world, and Bayliner decided to produce a fishing boat called the Charlie White Special. "I gave them some ideas, but they came out with a boat with just a downrigger hooked onto it. I didn't think it was very special. 'You have to design it right,' I told them, 'with fish boxes and a well to store bait.' This became the Trophy, which started out as 16- and 18-foot boats, then grew to a 28-footer. I have one down at the dock."

Charlie firmly believes that any new product must solve a problem. He observed, for example, that many people he took fishing didn't know how to keep a fish on the line after it struck. "It used to drive me absolutely nuts because I'd take people out, they'd hook the fish and lose it, and at the end of the day, they'd blame me. So I asked myself, 'What actually happens underwater? How do fish act around a lure?'" To answer those questions, he attached an underwater camera to the downrigger. The resulting video, which showed how a fish approaches and strikes a lure, became a hit. A skilled showman who loves talking to audiences, Charlie rented Vancouver's Queen Elizabeth Theatre, told jokes and showed his film. He repeated the presentation 10 times. The Seattle Opera House was next, then theatres all over California. The film was more than entertainment. The underwater camera showed how often a fish would bite, then open its mouth and spit out the hook. That led to Charlie's developing an electric hook sharpener. "The hook has to be sharp enough to stick on your fingernail," he says with emphasis. "If it won't stick there, it won't pierce the bony surface of the fish's mouth. Sharp hooks will triple your catch."

The first video's success whetted his desire to know more about the life of fish in their habitat. Again deploying a remotely operated camera, this time from a ship in the southern Pacific Ocean, an energetic Charlie, with a rather wild thatch of greying hair, filmed the rovings of the great white shark. He also shot the movements of a herring ball, with its millions of individual fish swimming in unison. The herring form schools to repel predators, a technique that's only partially successful: gulls attack from above; common murres — resembling high-speed penguins when diving — herd the herring and nip individuals at the ball's edges; salmon attack like a wolf pack, swimming right through the ball with mouths wide open; and humpback whales feed exclusively on herring, swallowing the "silver darlings" by the thousands. These filming ventures led to a television series, *Charlie White's Underwater World*. Charlie has also shown his films and made presentations about underwater nature on cruise ships.

He shows me his "rogues' gallery," an alcove with photos of himself in the company of Kevin Costner, former B.C. premier Mike Harcourt, Andre Agassiz and David Foster, who composed the music for Charlie's television show. His framed "B.C. Sport Fishing Hall of Fame" certificate hangs next to a portrait of scientist Carl Sagan. He has fished with all of them.

In 2000, Charlie suffered a stroke that paralyzed his right side. With therapy, especially from his son David, a kinesiologist, he's again ambulatory, but the stroke made him aware of his mortality. Subsequently, he decided to do something significant for the community. He and Darlene donated time and money to the Saanich Peninsula Hospital's fundraising campaign and then made a $600,000 gift to Sidney's Sanscha Community Centre. In gratitude, the town named the centre's performance hall the Charlie White Theatre.

Although he may not walk at the same speed he once did, his inventiveness hasn't faded. He's working on the Forget-Me-Not, a tiny electronic device that can be attached to any object, even a person. "I've lost so many pairs of glasses," explains Charlie. "But with this gizmo, if I get farther than a certain number of feet away from my glasses, a battery-operated beltpack beeps and reminds me. It can be used to track a PalmPilot, attach to your laptop when you're going through airport security, even track small kids in the mall." He hopes to have the device on the market in the next year.

Electronic inventions don't keep Charlie from what he still finds irresistible. "Fishing has completely influenced my life. It prompted me to come to Oregon and then to British Columbia. My love of fishing has made me want to spread the word. I'm an evangelist for fishing. It's a great sport and I'm still fascinated by learning more about it and about all the life under the sea. I see teaching people how to fish as my legacy. It gives them lifelong recreation, but also an important survival skill. You know the old Lao Tzu saying, 'Give a man a fish, you feed him for a day; teach a man to fish, you feed him for a lifetime.'"

Marianne Scott is a columnist for *Pacific Yachting* and writes for numerous marine publications. She grew up in the Netherlands and came to North America as a teenager. She rediscovered her seafaring roots when she and her husband, David, sailed to Bora-Bora and back on their Niagara 35, *Starkindred*. She lives in Victoria, British Columbia, about 40 feet from Juan de Fuca Strait.